# The Kiss Of Life

in Poems by
Kevan Myers

Published by CompletelyNovel, 2018,
the new home of Dancing Yeti Books.

Copyright © Kevan Myers 2018

Kevan Myers has asserted his right under the Copyright, Designs and Patents Act 1988 to be identified as the author of this work.

Cover design by Karen (Rambha) Peck, Kevan Myers & Aruna Almaleh, with technical help from John Green and Will Parry. Yetis by D.R. Postgate. All cover photos of Dawn at Sri Arunachala, Copyright © Markus Horlacher. All rights reserved.

This book is sold subject to the condition that it shall not, by way of trade or otherwise, be lent, resold, hired out, or otherwise circulated without the publisher's prior consent in any form of binding or cover other than that in which it is published and without a similar condition including this condition being imposed on the subsequent purchaser

ISBN 9781787232983

Other Poetry from Kevan Myers:

Salvage From The Ark (1978)
Tasting The Spring Where Pictures Sing (2006)
Is (2009)

To place orders for these earlier books,
or to contact the author:

email: dancingyeti@gmail.com

# Contents

| | |
|---|---|
| vi | Dedication to one who gave life a long kiss |
| vii | Some Quotations |
| viii | Where thanks are due |

## Poems By Page & Title

| | |
|---|---|
| 1 | Invocation |
| 2 | The Kiss of Life |
| 3 | The Palette Lives |
| 4 | What Those Nature Flicks Don't Show |
| 5 | The First Wish |
| 6 | Speaking Beyond Words |
| 7 | Chucking The Crutches |
| 8 | The Usual Dilemma |
| 9 | Perception Of Perspectives |
| 9 | Round Sound Rhapsody |
| 10 | Digging |
| 12 | Earth |
| 15 | Epitaph....... |
| 15 | Palæolithic Pathos (R.I.P.) |
| 16 | The Kiss Of Death |
| 17 | This Peace Of My Heart |
| 18 | No Freehold Here |
| 19 | Welling Up In Carolina |
| 20 | Twelve Portraits of Water In One Stream |
| 28 | Herr Thor's Donation |
| 29 | A Trespass On Your moments |
| 30 | Back In The Beginning |
| 32 | On The News That Refugees Will Be Left To Drown |
| 35 | Turning Over The Welcome Mat |
| 38 | The Curse of Mirrors |
| 39 | Trapped By Glass |
| 40 | Peter Pan: My Kind Of Man |
| 42 | One Secret Delight Of Teaching The Arts |
| 42 | Confession |
| 43 | Inspirational |
| 44 | On Missing The Soul Of The Selfie |
| 47 | Thorts On Curators' Hottest Potatoes |
| 47 | Best Limerix |
| 48 | On Getting One's Ration Of Compassion |

| | |
|---|---|
| 49 | To Lay at the Feet of Dr Donne |
| 50 | The Limits Of Minutes |
| 51 | The Optimist |
| 52 | For Ludwig Van B And His Friends |
| 54 | Return Of The Prodigal |
| 55 | When Romance Was Tough |
| 56 | From Sleep to Wake |
| 57 | Only Now Matters |
| 58 | What Duty To Beauty? |
| 60 | ... and The Winner izzzzzzzzzz... |
| 64 | Uncivil Service At The Tulle Prefecture |
| 65 | Keeping It Dark |
| 65 | Here's A Marvel |
| 66 | Beep, Beep, Bloody Beep! |
| 67 | Bubble Hubble |
| 68 | London Encounter |
| 69 | A London Seen |
| 70 | Take Note, Throat |
| 72 | Baghdad Nightrise |
| 72 | In Tropic Climes |
| 73 | Where Seekers Seek & Gurus Sit |
| 74 | On Indian Time |
| 75 | Houses Of God |
| 76 | Hindu Temple |
| 80 | Blue Mosque |
| 81 | Song From A Minaret |
| 82 | Going To Church |
| 85 | Without The Holy Clothes |
| 85 | Settling In The School By The Fields |
| 86 | L'Église De St. Sylvain |
| 87 | Dry Haku |
| 87 | Wet Haiku |
| 87 | A Biblical View |
| 88 | Inside Stained Glass |
| 89 | What Is Masochism? |
| 89 | Bright Night Alleyway |
| 90 | *Some Shakespearean beginnings start with:* "A poor player who struts and frets . |
| 91 | Ingredients Of Mr Shakespeare's Recipe |
| 92 | No Pain In The Stain |

| | |
|---|---|
| 93 | The Way Of Untruth |
| 94 | Clocking In And Out |
| 96 | Pills for Ills |
| 97 | Knock Knock |
| 97 | Momentarily |
| 98 | Memoir To Myself |
| 101 | What's New? |
| 101 | The Joker Speaks |
| 102 | Here Be Tonics For Electronics |
| 104 | Close To The Home Of Friends |
| 105 | In An Alaskan Cabin |
| 105 | Nome Pomes |
| 106 | Where Patients Learn Patience |
| 108 | Being Supernaturally Yours |
| 110 | I Wandered Lonely As A Car |
| 112 | The Teaching Of Leaves |
| 114 | Where All Paths Meet |
| 114 | Horses |
| 115 | Train Faces |
| 116 | Soller to PalmaTrain 1980 |
| 117 | Deya, Majorca |
| 117 | As Time Goes By |
| 117 | Under Mulhaçen |
| 118 | The Last Haiku Master |
| 120 | Chinese Masterpiece |
| 120 | Insight |
| 121 | Letting Things Wait |
| 121 | Frogs |
| 122 | Wake Up In The Morning Poem |
| 123 | How It Was |
| 124 | Where's The Happy Ending? |
| 126 | Please Beguile My Smile |
| 126 | Being Human |
| 127 | Deconstructing |
| 128 | A Look At Life |
| 129 | Epilogue |
| 130 | *Afterword*: Why Poetry? |
| 132 | About the author |

## Dedication: To One Who Gave Life A Long Kiss

I dedicate these poems to a red-haired, madcap, Australian, called Keith Nightingale, because I remembered him as soon as I found the title: 'Kiss Of Life'.

One day, we'd just climbed out of the swimming pool, in the Lucknow forest, when we noticed a young Indian man was floating in the water, face-down .

So we pulled him out, and while our other friends backed off in horror, Keith surprised me by starting to give the 'kiss of life', and told me quickly how to pump the chest, to start the heart.

In the Indian sun, the body felt cold and slimy from the water. When we started work, a load of vomit came between the mouth to mouth, which would have driven me off the job, but Keith just spat sideways and continued.

So we worked on, getting more tired and sad at the lack of response, until we realised twenty minutes had passed and we had to stop, for the heart would not start. All the hope of youth had gone forever from this cold flesh .

We felt sorry we'd failed in this job, but I found I could not mourn for this unknown being, whose empty body had been left in our hands; though I felt sorry for the friends and family I'd never meet.

But we were alive and needed to clean off our sweat and re-connect with life, so we jumped back in the pool and had a swim; for the water that had drowned him was only water and carried no guilt.

And thus, so many years later, the determination and care that he showed that day, have come back to my mind. So here is my ode to Keith Nightingale and this book is dedicated to him.

A FewQuotations

"That Tao which can be put in words
is not the true Tao"

                 *Lao Tse*

"What's in a name? That which we call a rose
By any other name would smell as sweet;"

              *Juliet, (Shakespeare)*

The language I have learn'd these forty years,
My native English, now I must forego:
And now my tongue's use is to me no more
Than an unstringed viol or a harp,
Or like a cunning instrument cased up,
Or, being open, put into his hands
That knows no touch to tune the harmony:
Within my mouth you have engaol'd my tongue,
Doubly portcullis'd with my teeth and lips;
And dull unfeeling barren ignorance
Is made my gaoler to attend on me.
I am too old to fawn upon a nurse,
Too far in years to be a pupil now:
What is thy sentence then but speechless death,
Which robs my tongue from breathing native breath?"

      *Thomas Mowbray, on his exile by Richard II,*
                    *(Shakespeare)*

## Where Thanks Are Due

Being an isolated exile, living abroad by choice, I am glad that times have changed since Shakespeare wrote these lines, so I am able to use my own tongue though I live far from my native soil, where there are poetry scenes and readings, where works get tested and critical thoughts are sometimes offered.

I owe particular thanks to a few friends who've taken time to read my words and given the encouragement that brought me joy and the urge to keep them flowing.

Anjali Walsh has got me restarted on writing a few times when I thought the muse had departed forever; Karen (Rambha) Peck has helped design this book cover and given honest criticism. My sister, Kerris, has also given her views, which have helped me to edit my words.

There is also a group of exiles around the Department of Corrèze, in France, who meet together to write and hear each other's work, and many of these poems were written in their presence, which I value, for its support and encouragement, as well as their culinary skills, which have kept me from starving in my garret. In particular, I mention John Green, who helped me start up this group and has kept it vibrant with the wit and wisdom of his words.

I also thank a couple of departed beings: my father, Peter Myers, and my step-father, Oliver Postgate, who were not ideal dads; but they were both writers who revelled in the play of words, which is the joy of our language, and passed on to me their love of its subtleties, rhythms and rhymes.

# *The Poems*

## Invocation

The muse comes crashing through my door,
with boobs so full of images and rhymes
they soon may lose the fight to keep
her thumping heart inside.

"Get off your arse!" she screams,
while grabbing in her fists
the chatter from my radio, to twist
it into plaits to swing around her head
until she lets them go,
like slung-shot snooker balls, to boing
from side to side between
the unseen walls that try
to make the universe
stop jumping from the sky.

She sucks up every perfume found in space
and blasts them in my face, to shake
my lazy senses wide awake.

But can she break
the pile of rocks that blocks my brains,
to liberate the demons of my mind
and let them riot out and ride
to all the wild scenes she loves
where masterpieces hide,
and all the strength of me
must be entwined
to haul them by the souls
till they come bursting up, to bare
their perfect faces to the eyes.

I pray for magic cauldrons
where the liquids sing and shout
while all I need to be is fingers round a pen
to give the only gift I'm fit to give.

Perhaps I can.

## The Kiss Of Life

The kiss of Life
refuses all delay,
and tears apart
the packaging
which shields our lives,
in untamed haste to be
united with the I
behind the eye
that makes the earth and sky
the gateway to the next
unveiling gasp of breath.

So fill me, Life,
because I have no time
to wait for anything,
not even 'Now',
because it's running
out the door & gone.

Just kiss me with your lips
and I am born.

## The Palette Lives

The sun unsets
and colours run
down from the sky,
to change to fire,
water, and ignite
the slender arms of pines,

While faces, in its warmth,
transform to canvasses
that tempt the artist
to experiment, and find
new colours, yet unborn.

His brush gets busy,
touching up and stirring
out of sleep the dreams
displaced from night,
that splash like mermaids
through the rings
of lobster light, to sing
their tribute to the day.

The sun, that soon may rise,
is whisked with bits of cloud
into an omelette mix, and now
the cock a doodle sings, to say,
it's time again to take your part
on stage, and act the play.

## What Those Nature Flicks Don't Show

I read the words of Madge*,
that mighty poet, wrapped
in newspapers and coats, with eyes,
like giant windows to a world inside:
where forms are huddled round the fire,
so close it stings the flesh,
and nose runs with the stench
of scorching clothes,
surrounded by the hurtling clouds
that leap the tops of cliffs
like suicidal skies.

"I hope you get my drift,"
the glacier replies.

How long can icebergs live
when sunset turns the waves to flames
and polar bears are flayed
by streaks of pink,
while patiently they sit
by fishing holes and knit?

No seal's nose protrudes
for seal knows who's playing 'it'.

A line of penguins changes guard
to mournful notes, conducted by
the walrus's moustachios,
through which course tears and tears,
to soak each one of his abundant hairs;
where whales, stranded, dread
the well-intentioned hands
of interfering humans,
who would ruin their plans
to transit peacefully
according to the rites
laid down in ancient times
that brought them to these sites.

*Madge Herron, wild soul from Donegal, actress, great poet, friend to many animals, including me. Long may she rest in wonder.

How else can they come back
as peacock butterflies
to float in oh-so-much
-desired, tropic skies?

A writer has to raise a flipper
now and then, to mop his brow,
as chorus lines of Jersey cows
hoof "Knees Up Mother Moo"
on open meadows
basking in the shadows of horizon trees,
where sun unsets, as soil gently breathes.

## The First Wish

I've got to throw away this urge
to rhyme and sanitise my words
They must break out of safety's net
to shake their fists and bare their bums,
and shout, "to hell with it!
I will accept whatever comes."

## Speaking Beyond Words

The truth of things is wordless:
leaving mind struck dumb
and mouth left gasping
like a fish unhooked
and thrown on the bank.

Because there is
no man-made word
that can convey
the fullness of a thing,
that calls for every sense
to have its say.

The words we use
are nothing more
than symbols writ in sound
with no more power
to bring to life the "is"
than matchstick people
proudly standing
by their flowers,
with eight petals and a stem
before the front door
of their residence,
with its two windows
and the chimney,
with its smoke like cotton wool.

Our language, has not words enough
to bring across the miracle of things,
and even in the privacy of minds,
we can't escape the limits of the thoughts
that bind us to the past, with words
some other beings have made
because we are locked in
by gates which only will admit
the thoughts that fit
inside the boundaries
that they've already built.

We've lost the power to take
ourselves beyond these walls
and thus create
the unknown universe
where we might be
astounded by each moment
as it flies into our lives.

This language is a precious tool
that gives me power to share
some feelings and ideas,
but still it's just a metaphor
that's grasping for the real
touch of everything,
so far beyond  -so far before-
the power of words
to say a thing.


## Chucking The Crutches

"Can language stand
without its old familiar frame?"
I dare to ask
as my old nut un-nuts the bolts
and swaying, half-attached, is all.

Just watch my dance
before inevitable fall.

There's no escaping
from the axe,
but what a wild race
we'll have
when words untied
become my steeds,
and rainy pavements
open souls,
to suck my seeds!

## The Usual Dilemma

You've no idea how beautiful
the day out there,
which challenges my mind
that claims it wants to live
each moment of its life
with all my senses,
wide-awake and primed.

My body too
demands some movement
from my limbs,
before they seize from sitting
like a zombie in a chair,
with both eyes disappeared
inside a screen.

It seems my days
have dwindled down to here,
where I create
my chosen land,
unfound on earth
outside my mind,
and now transferred
through laptop to construct
this counterfeit of life,
to feed the greed
behind my eyes.

This battle between me and me:
(the one who sits
and he who craves to rise)
has now become the story of my life.

The winner and the loser of this fight
are both myself, of course:
a dual-natured Gemini.

## Perception Of Perspectives

I am still and do not move,
as I walk through the garden,
seeing the path unwind its scenery,
as it grows closer to the end
with every step
it wanders into me.

## Round Sound Rhapsody

The earth is spuds and clods
and clogs and bogs.
to sink with clotted hair
in muddy pie.

I croak, contented as a frog
beneath a looming sky,
too dark for crows to show,
except when in a yellow flash
they blink an eye
and caw me to the core,
where pale flesh
remains unborn,
and never found;
eternally vibrating
in a rattling growl
of holy sound.

Some call it 'Om',
but where's the path
and flowers that
I crayoned in before,
with mum and dad
and little me,
all smiling by the door?

## Digging

"The soil is rich," she said
and I believe, so dig and heave
at slabs of grass, and vines
all linked and intertwined
in one great fellowship of roots
determined to defy
the fork of any man who dares to try
to render them apart and raise them high.

But I
am in a fighting mood
and so I place my tines
squarely beneath,
the twined-up roots, and then
I bend my knees to be
defenders of my back,
as both my hands
lock on the shaft of fork,
to be my lever and my crane
as grunting manfully I try
to haul the clump straight up,
while fears of hernias
dig elbows in my mind.

It fights my strain at every inch...
until that moment when ...
it suddenly gives in,
as root to root lets go
and sends me stumbling back,
relieved and proud
that these old limbs,
much better used to pushing pens
around a desk, still have
enough of energy and strength
to triumph so Titanicly
in this Olympic tug of war.

I grab it by its grass and bash
its underside against my fork,
but still the sods of clay,
cling on with sticky hands, reluctant
to desert their home,
where now my tines
provide an anxious worm
a temporary roost, as I attempt
to shake the topsoil off,
to lighten up the pieces I must haul
to where my compost waits
to turn them back to soil,
with rockets in its cells
to give the seeds and roots
a mighty boot-up on their journey
into flowers and fruit.

But this will be a later job;
for now the scent of healthy earth,
exhaling to new air, comes welling up
and wreathes an ever-widening
smile on my face as I breathe deeply,
in my joy, at this new shaft
that leads direct to life,
in such a pulsing vein,
it only needs a pinch of seeds
to make the fireworks begin.

# Earth

My horoscope holds many signs
composed of fire and air,
while those of Mother Earth are rare.
Yet now it's she who brings me joy,
not from her sensual vales and hills, but bare,
and elemental, formed of broken
and discarded left-overs of life that rot away
to make themselves our sandstone and our clay.

I used to hate it when she clung on to my hands
and would not let them go
until she'd dried and shrivelled up my skin,
while nails would black and crack.
I'd run to soap and water, even cream,
that might revive this flesh
that seemed sucked lifeless by the lips
concealed in her touch. But now,
like some spent lover, they will rarely come
into my mind, when washing's done.

I'm glad to clamber down my path
and leave behind my problems, to attend
the meetings with my plants, where I
admire how tall this one has grown, close to
a brand-new bloom that's sprung,
or I may stumble on
some shy tomato's blush,
that's just begun.

But strangely, it is rare you'll find
me, hunkered down in bliss, among
the colours and the scents of all
these green and gentle friends,
though there be some
with jealous lovers
who will treat me to an itch, or bare
their thorns, to leave me stung.

They seem to me like neighbours who stick heads
outside their doors to nod as I come sniffing by,
en route to one, who beckons me,
with new and lovely face, where I
will bend or kneel, uncomfortably,
but rarely sit, beside its bed, for company.

I move among them more as midwife, or as doctor,
than as guest: alert to changes in their form,
amazed by speeds of weeds, who clamber up
like muscular marines: ascending ropes,
to shove themselves ahead and jump the queue
that's climbing for the sky,
engrossed in stealing all the food,
intended for these weaker immigrants,
transplanted to their land, and questioning
who let them trespass here.

And what is this usurping hand,
who tears them struggling from their home
to fill it with these guests, so useless and effete
they barely would survive without its help,
to satisfy their thirst with drownings that defy
the rhythms that give meaning to the sky.

Each morning I explore, and it is like the time
I dwelt close to the Kentish shore,
where giant mud-flats bare themselves
and never is there stillness,
free from change, for all the time
the tide runs in or out, alive
with hues that swirl, as sun and moon
revolve their giant eyes
on waves and mud that sink and rise.

All things reshape as fast as breath,
propelled by clumsy feet and hands
of humankind, that interfere,

while they themselves
are changed to someone else,
a step ahead on their long journey
from crustacean into man, and then
to God knows what...

This movement never dies
and always has the power to surprise
when nature sheds the clothes
that had concealed change,
and blatantly reveals
her readiness to reproduce
with stamens that excite
like pheromones, with deep
enticing perfumes, while the petals lure
with pulsing shades that trap the eyes.

I must thank God
she has consented and been trained
so subtly to engage herself
with hands as ignorant as mine
that have no more than one
green finger out of ten.

She knows that I mean well;
though bramble-scratched and old
and aching from my work,
she does not kick me out,
but lets me be her mate.

Then here, on this truly varied bed,
of beauty and of pain,
we procreate.

Epitaph to be carved on my tombstone,
intoned as my ashes are laid to rest,
and plainsung a thousand years, in a
chantry, manned by a monkish choir

"See ya later, Alligator"


## Palaeolithic Pathos (R.I.P.)

Dumb, as deep in rocks,
untouched by daylight,
silence sleeps
in such a peace,
an ear that spent
a million years
tracking the ground
could not pick up
the rustle of a leaf.

Now, breath-held, bone-filled
silence of a pit, holds sad,
two skulls and spines declined
and pillowed in the clay.

Their finger-bones
are delicate like those
of kangaroos who never knew
one leap could carry them
into their last, unfathomable sleep.

Here they remain,
a weight of tons
that's piled in a heap.

## The Kiss Of Death

Dark clouds are chased across an angry sky,
and I, without a face, refuse to turn
towards the blazing eye
that stares across the universe, to pry
into the drapes that mask the empty core
inside my changing shape.

These smoking-dregs of me
can only find security, within the stained
and threadbare rag that is my hood,
which floats above the cloak
that shrivels from the earth
as my two fleshless arms,
unwearied, wield
the dripping scythe.

I'm chained by clockwork;
tightly wound by its great key,
enmeshing me, in this long groove
carved out of time, from which I cannot move
aside and hide, as scene by scene, I ride,
suppressing every feeling
that would make me smile or weep,
as I drive on to my next rendezvous,
and slash on either side,
the peaceful, with their smiles, anæsthetised,
and those aghast, who try to run and hide.

I come to bring relief: for time
dictates the moment that must be.
It is no choice of mine. But to transgress,
an instant overtime would drag the stars
beneath the ground and blow
the whole eternity down one black hole,
where even I can't go.

So many I have freed
from their imprisonment in flesh.
I feel them all, around me, making one,
no more divided, lost and ripped apart,

as though they fill the space
that once contained my heart
with rays of some forgiving sun.

No arm conducts the symphony
through which they flow,
which changes instantly,
mysterious in swirls,
astonishing each moment,
with the beauty that it is,
which cannot be, without my scythe
to make it so.

For who would have the endlessness
of age and rot, if I were not?
Who could aspire to rise,
without somewhere to go?
They plead with me: "Not now;
I have so much to do!"
because they cannot see
they stand before a truck
which cannot slow,
because it has no brakes.

It is not me behind the wheel,
but I know, too well, those hands
may leave you maimed in living hell.
And so I shear you swiftly as I can
to clasp you in the space of my embrace
and only wish that you'd respond
and take my hand,
to show me that, at last, you understand.


## This Peace Of My Heart

Total unbreath is death
as boom dee-dee boom
turns in for doom....

## No Freehold Here

I thought to make
this corner of the World, my own,
but ownership can never be reality
while men are made of skin and bone.

I cannot truly call this body "me".
It is a temporary home,
that stands on sand
beside a changing sea,
where what I am
in stillness, is,
unlimited by any thing,
without the need of lips to sing.

An accident of birth
attached some labels to my being
without my choice,
but there have been some times
when I have proudly brandished them
to celebrate some victory in war,
or, on a field, some sporting feat
that's only given prominence,
because the pressmen need to eat.

Such stuff is fluff
that disappears as easily as flesh
melts off the bones,
when all this me
I've made myself, is done
and on this nothing rises
nothing like the sun.

Yet still there is
this deeper me,
unmade by anyone,
that nothing is,
which has no end
and never has begun.

## Welling Up in Carolina

This spring
is the voice of the earth.

Lips of clay,
bubbling forth,
sing

as tiny bits
of sand and pebble
dance
in underwater
swirls

like spinning
dervishes,
or girls

in whirling
petticoats
of bubbling pearls.

The light of sky
has plunged inside
this mirror,
where its wistful eye

looks back
with no nostalgia
for the height
from which it dived,

for here inside
these waves,
so fresh and new,

it's realised the dream
of every
drop of dew.

## Twelve Portraits Of Water, In One Stream

1. **The** voice of the waters
   is hard to ignore.
   It sings us to smiles
   or scares us with roars
   as its battering fists
   beat wild on the rocks,
   or rear up in madness
   and tear down our doors.

   Like a chattering friend
   who shortens the road,
   it gabbles and sings
   at our side as we mount
   to the underground spout
   where it first bubbles out,
   so clean and so cold,
   like a ghost in a pond,
   or oozing its way
   to the air, from the clay...

   Some ripples begin
   in places untrod,
   where drops
   turn to trickles
   which murmur or slop,
   or they ooze from the squelch,
   where they bubble and belch
   from spluttery lips,
   more like anus than mouth,
   and no-one is wise
   to what heavens they've kissed
   before they piss down
   out of storms, or they drift,
   as softly as feathers,
   in kiss of the mist.

2.  *Th*ey fall out of silence,
    while some ring like bells
    with voices in chorus
    that murmur then swell,
    as they criss and they cross,
    some singing some lost,
    like the grains from the rocks
    that they toss in the waves.

    And the grass on the banks,
    has to give up its hold,
    as the earth from its roots
    is dispersed in the flood,
    while it shoves through the narrowest
    gap between shores,
    till it meets with the brink,
    where it falls with a roar
    and is lost in a mist
    that drenches the air,
    where shafts of the light
    that springs from the sun
    make rainbows that colour
    the drops of the dark,
    where rock-faces meet
    and embrace in their arc.

3.  **But** we must climb wide
    for the rocks are too steep
    for a path to descend
    straight down to its deep.

    So we trail around,
    with our ears open full,
    for it's grown so quiet
    we hush any speech,
    as we scrape through the branches
    to find where it lies,
    scarcely moving, in calm,
    and flat on its back,
    tattooed by the shadows
    and flickering rings,
    where the fishermen squint
    at their floats that are spun
    through the fragments of gold
    that are thrown by the sun.

    ~~~~~~~

4.  **It** laps at the wharves
    and the quays at the feet
    of riverside houses
    with backs to the street.

    ~~~~~~~

5.  **While** the patter of raindrops
    calls eyesight to shift
    its focused attention
    to water that twists,
    like a rope down the glass
    till its split-ends unite
    into puddles that hang
    till their globules undam,
    and once more they flow
    to the pavements below,

through the cracks in the paintwork
and down to the drains,
where the trash starts to nudge
then lets go with a rush,
till it bruises and shoves
like a runaway train.

~~~~~~~

6.  **N**ow it slows to a chug
    like the barges that bob
    in the wake of their tug,
    or the cygnets who follow
    behind Madame Swan.

    Its rhythm grows slow,
    as the flotsam and moon
    that are floating past lights,
    that are strung from the wires,
    like stars on the swell,
    and the colours that change
    as they govern the roads,
    which reflect on the darkness
    that laps at the steps,
    so far from the fields
    and leaf-dappled shade
    where the cows came to cool
    in the heat of the day.

    ~~~~~~~

7.  **I**'ve stood by many waves,
    and run from them, then stood again
    with sand that trickles
    through my toes, once I
    have gone beyond
    the sucking of the ooze
    beside the slime that yearns
    to skid me to a crash, on buried rocks,
    that lie in wait, to jar my bones.

8. ***T**he sea is never still.*
   It fills the eyes and dreams
   of waking minds,
   with changing shapes,
   like streaks of paint
   that whirl and sweep
   round half-seen things,
   with huge, sad, knowing eyes,
   or streamlined shapes that fly
   through waves, or underneath;
   while others grub around
   like mud with legs, or whiskery
   and curled up things,
   that turn into embarrassed pink
   when heated up...
   then cooled ... to lie,
   with beady eyes,
   beside the drink.

   ~~~~~~~

9. ***T**he sea can be*
   a grunting, howling monster
   full of moods and threats, it hides
   among deceptive joys, it uses to entice
   and lure us, running to its reach
   when we've been burning on its beach.

   While winds conspire to change
   its placid face, to overbites
   that teeter on each peak,
   about to roar,
   and gnash the cliff,
   or drop its load, to squirm
   and squiggle on the shore

10. ***Its*** voice can be
the sound that rules your life.
A fisherman once asked me,
"Can you hear it?"
"What?" I asked.
"The voice," he said,
"The singing of the sea.
I never have, because
it's always been too close to me."

"My daughter wed a farmer,
with a house far from the coast.
I went to stay,
but had to leave
the second day.

Because I felt all wrong:
without its song,
I thought that I was ill,
and could not sleep, or even
stay a moment, still."

It's different for me.
I have not dwelt long on the shore,
and now I'm far inland;
but when I lean out of my door,
the singing of the stream,
below me in the valley,
never leaves
and when my mind and ears
are listening,
I think all beings
must hear this voice
and even closed-up minds
must smile when it calls.

11. **But** then tsunamis
    burst into my thoughts,
    with all those corpses and those cars
    they throw about and strand
    so many tens of miles inland .

    I think of rains that will not stop,
    until the dams must open wide their doors,
    and waist-high waters fill
    suburban sitting rooms,
    with News-time camera work
    of grannies with their cats
    beleaguered on their roofs.

    And don't we smile, and love it too,
    to see this war-time chaos
    bring its thrills to our TVs
    and flush away their day to day routine,
    where soaps are yawning from the screen ,
    not frothing round our three-piece suites.

    There's nothing like a deluge
    for exciting shots of homes
    and churches: so much more
    romantic, as they mirror on the waters
    where the postman rows his rounds.

12.  **A**nd even that great seething tide
of floating cars, or battered shacks,
cannot be wild, or strange enough
to satisfy our greed to find
the most gigantic waves.

It seems we cannot wait until the moon
comes nestling up so close
it drags our waters into one
gigantic spout, to suck the oceans dry,
before delivering its final clout,
while every other sound
gets drowned,

As we, last,
fascinated beings
come out to greet our fate,
while Noah's last descendant
lifts his glass
to toast the present and the past,
then pours it down.

## Herr Thor's Donation

Under thunder,
things diminish.

Every other voice
is hushed
and lesser lights are crushed
by this untrammelled

oathing of the skies
that beats like madmen
on the drums
inside the ears
behind our eyes.

While up on high
the sky is torn apart
by jagged rips
of naked force,
like white-hot ice,
that sear a zigzag
through the turmoil
of this mid-day night

to knife into
the eye-ball of the world
and shake all things
from their accustomed place.

The flooding sky
is gashed by life,
untouchable and pure,
and every solid thing
is insecure.

## A Trespass On Your Moments

I haven't done what I oughter done,
and there's no good in me,
beneath the sun, but that which sprung,
unsown and unhoed,
from out my earth.

I never made request
that songs be sung to celebrate
the strainings of my birth.

I think I have no choice
except to carry on
with my undoings,
and the screwings
and unscrewings,
which have been
ordained by Mother Earth

The dance of life
goes reeling past the snores,
and I-pad addicts
lost in mental wanks,
as tube trains sway and rumble
through the blanks
inside the tunnel,
till they blunder out beneath
the undreamed skies,
which split and run
as all the sewn up things
become undone.

Indeed, the hour has come
to fold up time
and have some fun.

## Back In The Beginning

How was it when we first began?
They tell me we are largely
made of water, after all.

And out of waves we came,
to wriggle on the beach,
to gasp the salted air,
and seek for shelter,
long before the power of thought
would come, to ask
why we were there,
or what it was had made us leave
the safety and the comfort
of our old home in the deep.

Were we escaping from the jaws
of some great beast?
Or did we just flounder
too close to the shore,
to be scooped up by combers
and hurled on a cliff
with bodies too weak
to return to the drift
and the music of waves?

It could be we'd burrowed
deep down in the mud,
when out went the tide
that was dragged by its feet
so far down the beach
that on its return
it had lowered its reach,
to leave us marooned,
too high and too dry,
to slide back to the deep,
to lie there confused
by the sand and the sky.

Whatever it was that bewildered our eyes
the song of the seas would be a surprise.

For down in the deeps
where the whale-songs boing
with echoes and bleeps
as the foreground to roars,
where shingle is hurled
in great scoops on the shores,
the voice of the waters must often be drowned
by such a gigantic confusion of sound.

Perhaps we just blundered onto some beach,
as high up the stream
as our bodies could reach,
before we collapsed into marshes or ponds
where we wriggled or flopped
as we sploshed in the mud,
where we strove to escape
and fought with our fins
until they transformed
to a landlubber's limbs,
with which we could crawl
away from the shore,
where predators' beaks
might devour the weak.

And after some æons
it must have been here
some natural genius
conceived the idea
of a beat of our own, beside
the tom-tom of the waterfall,
and slip-slap of the tide:
our feet could stamp the ground
and we could shout
and beat a drum,
to bring the news
to all the seas and earth,
that we, their true-born lords,
had come.

*From 2014 to now, I have been appalled by the news that thousands of refugees are drowning in the sea, while rich nations, like mine, slam the doors in their faces.
I wrote two poems about it and I offer both:*

## On The News That Refugees Will Be Left To Drown
### *(This day of shame, 28 October 2014)*

There's always a reason to keep them out.
"Our country's too full...
They're different...
they don't understand our way of life...
They'll work for cheap. They'll take our jobs.
Our wages will go down."
and every one of these beliefs may be the truth.

But off the coast of Italy
where sunbeams sparkle
on the crests of azure waves,
humans of every size and age
are fighting to find breath
that does not slurp more salt
into their mouths which slowly sink
or float in death.

Bodies of those who sailed out,
crowded in death-trap boats,
because they'd had enough
of wounds and pain, down every street,
around the now-deserted shells
that once were homes.

Bodies of those, whose lifeless eyes
had seen so much of fear and rape,
of terror, or disease,
that they had found the courage
to expose their families
to endless miles, set about by thieves,
where those, most weak, might fall
beside the road, like those
survivors of the camps,

who in the last days of the Reich
were forced on endless marches,
with the aim that none survive.

Many are victims of war,
whose only hope has brought them
to the beaches, half alive;
assisted by cthe poor and simple people,
much like them: for who, confronted,
face to face, by such a tragedy, could turn
their heart to stone,
like we do, safely lodged at home?

This very day, the news informs me
that the governments of the rich
and peaceful lands of Europe
have decided that their ships
which have patrolled the straits
to rescue drowning human beings
have been commanded
to return to port and let them die.

So thus each body lost
or washed ashore may speak
out of their voiceless mouths
to those who hope to join their search for life,
that they should stay just where they are,
or start the long trek back through Hell
in hope a few might just survive.

And thus our satisfied MPs
may gain a few more votes from those
who live in comfort with their lives,
who'd rather send some pennies
to a 'worthy cause' than open up their doors
to all that pain outside.
For none of us is ready to accept the blame
for, after all, each one of us is only one
among our many neighbors
who must feel the same.

But I remember well the millions who died
of famine in Bengal, while we were still in charge;
the countless Irish dead, when their potatoes rotted
and our English gentlefolk evicted them because
they had no pennies left for rent.

And I remember all those Jews
that we would not admit
when they were beaten robbed and killed
because they weren't 'the master race'.
although of course we weren't to blame!
For nobody invited them
to choose our door to knock.

So why is it their heaped up bodies
trouble us so much?
We were not guilty of this crime.
We just stood by and would not let them in.
Far better they should stay outside
then bring their foreign ways
inside our comfortable lives,
where, after all, we had no room.

And clearly nothing's changed
as we're prepared to slam the door again
and let another load of people die.
So long as we don't have to meet them
face to face and eye to eye?

I know each one of us belongs to our own tribe,
but we are past the stage
of cowering inside and hurling rocks.
We have enough to spare a bit and share
with those in utter misery.

If we must lock our doors
I'd rather take my stand outside and be,
alongside human beings,
who still can understand
the meaning of the word: 'humanity'.

## Turning Over The Welcome Mat

How can I know how it feels
to be another being than me?
To slip on the flesh of another
and feel life's joy and its cruelty
when land and sea combine
to make one cruel enemy?

The news is filled with views
of dinghies, designed
for a beachside splash
for a couple or two, now crammed
with bodies, rush-hour-jammed,
too tight, and too afraid, to move.

As seas slurp up and swirl
around their knees,
their souls in terror plead
to God to let them be
among the winners of this lottery
which reels in the saved
like gasping fish
who course their way
between the bodies of the drowned,
like human garbage, on the sea.

The blank and staring eyes
of those who only yesterday
sat round the fire to share
their stories and their hopes.
Now glassy-eyed, with faces
facing down, they float.

And water that was kind:
the answer to their prayers
in lands of drought,
has now become
an oceanful of tears
that batters them about
and swallows up their babies
with its greedy mouth.

There is no way for me
to be inside their skins
nor would I be, for I
am not some altruistic saint
who looks for pain to mortify his frame.
I do not seek the agony
from knives that pare the flesh
to slice from me my children and my wife.

Although the TV shows it me
I do not have capacity
to feel how it is when walls
begin to shake and giant slabs
of roof come crashing down.
Nor can I tell the sadness
when the history and beauty of a sacred place
is utterly extinguished and dispersed as dust.

Can rape be less a violation and a pain
when one poor, helpless daughter
feels it again, again?
My ears have never been
where shots and screams
come rattling at my door.

Where children sleep in peace
or quarrel over toys, how can I know
the desperation that will drive
a family to drag their limbs
through countless miles, lined
by vultures who will snatch with greedy beaks
each item and each being
that they love and keep,
in hope that some last fragments of their past
might still be with them as they try
to find some way between
the nightmares that lay siege to sleep.

I only know that when I was
a traveller in their lands,
where I, unarmed, alone,
could be so easily attacked and robbed

there always was some door that opened up
some friend I'd never known
who asked me in and gave me food.

And some of those same people,
or their friends, or kin,
are now among those bodies
that have been exposed
to every danger, waiting on the shore,
or standing on some fragile raft,
with water rising round their knees,
where only sea birds hear their final prayers
as they go down in grief.

And we would slam the door
through which they hope to come,
because our comfort might be threatened
by a family who speak our language strangely
or is clothed in different coloured skin,
who seek to work or find a home,
which gives security and peace.

What reason can there be
to justify this fear and lack of trust
that makes us stuff our ears
and pull the zips across our eyes?

Each one of those outside is me,
yet so much more, for they
already have survived so many lives in one,
while I have dealt with trivialities
which cannot be compared with all
that they've experienced and done.

It was John Donne who said
that 'no man is an island entire of itself.
For if a clod be washed away
then Europe is the less.'
And when that clod is washed from Asia
or from Africa it matters just as much.

With every human being that drowns
a member of my family goes down

## The Curse of Mirrors

The curse of mirrors compels me
to look at the things, to check if today
my face is more baggy, my hair more grey.

There are mirrors I hate
because I am sure
they will always distort
the beauty I'd hoped
would shine through my thought.

They smugly make sneers
at my wobbling guts
and diminish my parts
to a bean with two nuts.

They waggle their fingers from safe in their glass,
as I stomp away glad I'm unable to see
the unfocused blob that I think is my arse.

It's the most modern ones that bare me the worst,
with their horrible lighting, too bright or too dark,
that make me a ghost or a sinister shark.

It's long over time that we quickly returned
to that world where our features
remain half-discerned,
in the blade of a knife
or a glistening lake,
where placid reflections
can put you at ease,
always hinting at depth
with some well-placed trees;
forming indeed an unbeatable place
to peer at this mask of a well-worn face.

Such are the woes of one who's not
the lovely Lady of Shalott.

## Trapped By Glass

I'm caught like a dove,
who beats on the mirror,
consumed with love
for this being more perfect
than any, he's met or seen,
on all the branches of his life
on all his dances through the skies.

Each movement he would make
reveals itself, alive
before his eyes,
in perfect time
with every
impulse of his mind.

His longing makes him beat
like mad,
for every tap
is answered,
as this beak
comes just as fast, to meet
his own, that's maddened
more and more,
as he keeps trying to reach
this other part of him,
so luring and so sweet.

He feels the hurt
as much within
his being, as the bruises
in his flesh, that jar
each time he tries in vain:
yearning to share the perfect song
that lies beyond the pane.

## Peter Pan: My Kind of Man

In my unpleasant kind of school
where little boys transform
to little prefects who lay down the rules,
beyond a certain age
or size, you're meant to leave
your happy childhood behind
and change to little men.

And this is symbolised
by trousers, long and grey,
which itch your thighs
and heat your loins;
at odds you'd think
with warnings of the dire
consequence of sin
when such a heating up
may stretch your skin.

But bugger that,
I'm happy in my shorts
and socks, although they tend
to race between my left and right
to be the first to leave my knees
and make the speediest descent,
until they roll themselves in ease,
and give me comfort and content.

I loathe the hairy, itchy touch
of those grey-flannel trouser things, as much
as bathing trunks made out of soggy wool
that grab my crutch in such a nasty grip
they turn my thing
to half an inch of pale string.

So when I'm summoned to the Head,
and face to florid face with him
inside the stinky pipe smoke
of his horrid bristly room,
where he demands the reason why
I'm still in shorts, at thirteen years,

my panic makes me dive into my thoughts
to find the fastest smart reply
to free me from this penury.

So knowing that my parents
rarely pay his bills
I tell him that we lack
the funds to buy long trousers
and my legs are happy as they are.

At which he snorts,
"We can't have that!"
and clambers up the stairs
to fetch a pair
his son has worn
which he declares
can now be mine.

As if I'd clothe myself in cast-off,
hairy rags his whey-faced,
ape-like clone has cast aside,
when I have got at home a pair,
that I've ordained I'll never wear!

But now he's given me no choice,
so I must itch and sweat
with legs inside this prison,
with the wind and sun outside.

And soon my legs will be
as pale and ghostly
as the limbs that hang
beneath old men,
you only glimpse
between the turn-ups and the socks
at bus-stops,
or on buses when you sit
behind a creased,
and wrinkled neck,
that will no doubt
be forced upon me too,
before I'm through.

## One Secret Delight Of Teaching The Arts

"I love his work. It is
so inspirational!"

Her perfumed words
breathe in my ear,
still fresh from the depths of her soul,
while one pneumatic mammary reclines
upon the less-than-Harris tweed,
which clothes my less-
than-lumberjack épaule.

## Confession

I really have nothing to say,
and said it for years
while nobody hears.

Even my mind,
only pretends,
to live in this time,
where it's rattling
the door that won't let it in
for it's only allowed
to look at 'Now'
when the moment has gone
and dropped behind.

But the me,
who holds the key, is lost
in the world of the rain,
turning my eyes to drops
which bend and extend
until they let go
and escape
the invisible bonds
of my pane.

## Inspirational

"He's real inspirational," she said,
"You have to meet."

So I regard myself and ask
if such a rendezvous will be a treat
or more an uphill task.

I see his glowing cheeks
come through the door
to reverential hush
and then he mounts
his special seat,
where flowers are hung
around his neck,
while he begins to gush
about his power to conquer death
and how surrender to his touch
will set the whole world free.

Except for me!
For I am battling mental chains,
restraining me
from climbing on the stage
to tighten up the garlands round his neck
and run an instant check
on his mortality.

I guess my forebears
must have been a grunty lot,
too busy with their lives
to take a bath in holy smoke, or vibes
that claim to wash away
their dirt and sins.

And thus it's no surprise
that I go running for fresh air
between the 'oohs' and 'ahs'
and thunderous applause;
despite my urge to taint the scene
with roaring farts or snores.

## On Missing The Soul Of The Selfie

'Do I want to take a selfie?'
is the question I now face.
Is it vanity's inversion, or its proof
that I am so aloof
when others shove
these portraits of themselves
before the wide-eyed peepers
of the human race?

To tell the truth, although in certain lights,
and carefully arranged,
my looks may not appear too grim,
and sometimes I will gurn*
before my looking-glass
to see what monsters I can make
from my slack jowls and baggy eyes,
in general, I'm inclined
to neigh and rear,
when cameras try to freeze my face
and take it off somewhere..

I have not learnt the knack
of saying "cheese" in any way
that does not look as though
it's torture that has prised
my lips apart, to give this horrid view
of crowns and dentures,
blessedly concealed
when happiness creates
a natural smile on my face.

I see it as an act of war
when so-called friends expose
my blemishes to all, who tap
on their computers to reveal this form,
which startles, even me, from time to time,
as I pass glass, like mirrors,

*make faces*

which reveal my faults, with warts 'n all,
so clearly underlined, that I
will shy away, as though The Flying Scotsman
steamed into my field, with kilt awry,
to frighten off my dreams of oats
and comely mares, in years gone by.

In youth, I learnt it rude, to force
on family and friends,
albums filled with cheesy smiles
or slides that ran for hours
before they'd end.

I also well recall my inward sneer, before
the smartphone selfie first arrived,
watching this woman try to take
a portrait of herself before
the peak of Mt McKinley,
rearing high, above the clouds,
and her uninteresting head,
as she tried out her poses,
with tormented brows.

She worked on it for minutes while I stared,
unchivalrous, and too condemnatory
to volunteer my services,
to ease her care,
by helping her provide
this priceless proof that she was there.

But now I find I'm questioning
my prejudice and sneers
and wondering whyI am so sure
that it is much more safe to hide
than to expose myself,
by posing for those eyes,
with better sights to see,
that surely will not
empathise with unappealing me.

For certainly the choice
will be my own, on whether
I expose it to my friends, and after all,
self-portraiture has long
been so esteemed that galleries
are filled with artists' works,
that help us stare
into this other age,
where they have bared
some fraction of their souls.

However, when I prowl
the National Portrait Gallery,
it's not the browning visages
of proud Victorians
which hold my gaze;
for I am much more drawn
to modern works, which put both eyes
on one side of the face,
or contour it through wild daubs
and shapes, to speak
of all the things that make
the picture of this being, unique.

And thus I'm double trumped
for if I deign to make a selfie,
there are ways enough,
with Photoshop, for me to be
my own Picasso, Braque, or Scarfe,
by crafty tweaks of shapes,
to so distort the face,
that it draws eyes,
to dive inside,
and know the soul of me.

But nonetheless, I hope
the influence of Bacon,
or formaldehyded sheep,
will stay away,
when first I take my selfie,
then begin to play.

## Thorts on Curators' Hottest Potators

Conceptual art means
no more than a fart
in a field of beans;
no less than the stress
that furrows my brow,
believing there lies
an answer in Now,
while I am forever
surrounded by Then.

Though maybe the answer lies
at the end of this line
that staggers
uncertainly
out of my pen.


## Best Limerix

A guru, who dwelt in Shanghai,
had an ego as small as his eye.
When folks would insist
that he seemed to exist,
he was sure they were telling a lie.

A health-conscious freak from Capri
would never drink coffee or tea,
preferring to sup
on herbs in a cup,
fermented in yesterday's pee.

Two randy young maidens from Kent
met two lovely boys with a tent,
but in spite of their vamping
the boys went on camping,
and even the tent pegs were bent.

## On Getting One's Ration Of Compassion

The sufferings of one
can grip a million.
And that is how the media stay rich
From Auschwitz to Big Brother
there are fans with lots of cash.

So why spend time and money
making thrillers or sci-fi,
when starving Africans oblige,
and murderers and rapists
stretch our eyes,
to open up our pockets
for the products
we will buy to bring relief
from viewing all these sights
that bring us grief?

For purses, once unzipped
for charity, may buy
us lots of comfort stuff
to bring us compensation
for the sufferings we feel as we stare,
indignantly, from armchairs,
as the News once more reveals
the latest views of Hell

It almost seems bad manners
here to point this out
and break into the sympathetic
anger and the grief,
as tears roll down one cheek,
while fascination grabs
our other eye so well.

This is our nature, so
there doesn't seem much point
in making this complaint,
except perhaps that seeing this truth
may wise us up to who we are,
who's not the saintly being,
that we ain't.

## To Lay At The Feet of Dr Donne

The soul may be invisible, and yet
it is the part of you I find
inside my mind, when thoughts descend
the path through time
to where you played your part in mine.

Your face and movements, now are blurred,
with just a trace to speak
the outside form of you,
that caught my eye,
but these impressions fly
like paper in the wind,
around this peaceful centre of the storm,
which is the unseen being of you:

This part, which animates
the sparks of life and ever is,
whatever may sweep by
as time's unfriendly scissors snip.

There is and never will be
any disconnection,
where the need for touch
is just the gilding on a brush
for what already is so whole.

I cannot rip you from myself
for nothing would be left
but emptiness, so total,
no big bang could set
the void alight.

Without the soul
there's nothing here, but night.

## The Limits Of Minutes

I don't give a damn how old I am.
In fact I do not know.
The calendar may rule the length of days,
and when you tally them
perhaps they give an age
that you may pin on me,
but I am clearly free,
unless I choose to be their slave.

The mirror shows a face
they say is mine,
but I who live inside
have never been imprisoned
by the hands of time,
so mathematic in their pace.

They have their place
for catching trains
and honouring our dates,
because we need
agreement when to meet,
but what I bring along
and you, as well, I hope,
may be set free from cells or bars
constructed by those hands,
forever trapped inside
each ticking of the clock.

This being I am, existed
long before the strange idea of time
moved in, to occupy
the passing thoughts,
and locked them up
in dreams of being a mind,
that feels itself to be
the slave of bones and flesh
that traps the heartbeats in a net,
and chains them to mortality.

I am not it, though it seems part of me.
I range from age to age,
to peer into infinity of space,
or find myself once more
a babe being given suck,
or most of all, the silent sense
that what I am is nothing
that was ever sewn inside a form and stuck.

This being is unlimited and free
and this is so, although
sensations send their messages from all
the different regions that appear to be
the physical existence of a body
known as me, which changes day to day,
as some new bits are born.
while others fall away.

This being I am, is way
beyond the scalpel's probe
and there's no x-ray of the body
or the mind that can reveal
the truth of me, that even I will never know
but it is here, millennia beyond
the groping hands of time,
forever now, forever so.


## The Optimist

Trying to catch
The Moment,
I am lying in wait,
brimful with hope,
and Nothing for bait.

## For Ludwig Van B and His Friends
*(Jeroen van der Wel & Giovanni Carilli)*

These sounds invade the space
where I most safely am myself,
with signs hung on my doors
that say, "Do not disturb
my petty grunts and snores."

They penetrate the walls of thought
which are my last defence
to grab me by my soul
and drag it out, blindfolded, as it gropes
for words that might purvey
these pictures which invade
the hugeness of the space
behind my eyes.

I cannot hold them still enough
to tread across their span
to solid ground where I might try
to understand the feelings that they make,
and try in vain to find
a way to speak the wild waves,
and colours,
in the forms that they create.

I'm stunned that such a music
was conceived within a cave, made numb
by ears, so deafened by their drum
that anger might have been
the sole emotion that remained
to drown all remnant
of the joy and love
that still might flood that brain.

The two words 'deaf' and 'dumb'
march through our thoughts in pairs
and so we think where
no sound enters in
no sound may come,
and yet from out this head

there sprung this force
that tuned each
instrument to make
its journey in this way
that when they meet
their voices speak emotions
that no language made of words
could hope to speak.

I hear them reel and soar,
until they merge,
like oceans mingling
in the straits, where tides
march forward and retreat,
to carry us to shores,
where human feet
have never stood before.

The notes combine
to kiss and clash
among themselves, as
back and forth they dash,
or calmly float a while
before they helter off again, to leap
some yawning gap above the deep.

While I, bewildered in my joy,
can find no space to slide
my thoughts between
the heart of long dead Beethoven
and these great chords
which part the drapes
so we may glimpse the truth,
so full of sense that language
cannot start to climb this fence.

However much I try
to put in thought
the meaning of these sounds,
I'm like a child who's hardly learnt to be
yet tries to speak the meaning of the sea.

## Return Of The Prodigal

The moment he walks in,
a shudder shakes the room,
which scrapes the music to a stop
as though the needle has been knocked
to blindly bump across the track
and one by one, the eyes swing round,
like icicles, to dagger him.

They seem to slice
the flesh beneath the skin,
he'd fought for years, to toughen up,
to face the sadness and the shame
that made his name a word for sin,
once they had made
a scapegoat out of him
to bear all blame.

Perhaps it is insane: to risk
the hard-won layers of change
that could be torn and ripped away
to leave him, naked as a babe
unwanted and afraid.

But here he has to be, bewildered by
his choice, to face the cruelty
that has been made his destiny.

Some power has forced his feet
to march him back
to face this glaring light,
where now, his eyes can only see
her lovely presence there,
all dressed in white.

However she has flushed away their past
and washed her hands,
he still must make a way
between the shoulders and the hate
that blocks the path
to where he has to be,

although his legs are tottering,
half crippled by uncertainty.

He says, "I had to come,"
as she stands, smiling doubtfully,
with eyes that shine with tears,
and then she opens wide her arms
and tells him, "Welcome home."


## When Romance was Tough

1. Flowers dying in the hands
   of the man with Brylcreem
       in his hair.

   \*\*\*\*\*

2. Pockets full of sweat,
   stamping feet in snow,
   alone outside the cinema,
   the twentieth cigarette.


## The Wistfulness of Non-Trystfulness

Her body is long
and slim, as the fingers
which twist her frizzy hair,
to tuck some springy bits
behind her ear,
and give a view
between the fronds
of curling eyelash
where her eyes peep through.

I only wish they looked at me,
and not at you.

## Side Effect Of L'Amour

Smiling foolishly,
as dreams well up
and swirl
inside my head,
as though some Jesus
wandered by
and raised me from the dead.


## From Sleep To Wake

Waking is a mystery,
although at times
I slip from sleep so easily
it seems that I
have crossed no boundary.

But normally a wall
divides my woken self
from me a moment past,
in that deep land of dreams and snores,
and I am left no clue
why it should be that I,
just now, have broken through.

Is there a moment programmed into fate:
some time before the world began,
which hurls cold water at my brains
and bellows that it's time to wake?

I only know what brings me back
when outside sounds, or pre-set clock,
have opened up my eyes in shock,
or when the grumblings of my body
call me urgently to lose
the products of my food and booze.

I also wake because I am too hot,
or cold, it seems, but I'm not sure,
for such climatic changes
often start inside my dreams.

These are the known reasons
that will shake me up enough to leap,
or ghostlike, travel through
the walls of sleep,
but they are rare,
compared to all the times
I simply drift awake and unaware.

In first bewilderment and blur,
I sometimes take a while to recall
just who I am, and where, before I move
to pencil in my mind the list of stuff
I hope to do before this day is through.

And thus it stays a mystery to me
that I allow the day
to elbow me awake
and shake me from the rest
where I am so content to be
untroubled by the warp and weft
of this unreal web,
that traps this being called 'me'.


## Only 'Now' Matters.
### Bugger 'Then'!

If 'Now' is not all
it ought to be
there'll never be
hope for 'Then'.

It is always the same,
in the beginning and the end,
when it comes to that
which 'is',
but never 'was',
nor 'shall be'.

Amen

## What Duty To Beauty
*(a poem in 2 movements)*

It's clouds that bring
the special to my view
and turn it into wonderland,
transforming flat and blue
to toppling towers
thronged with light,
where colours dance
or rest,
in violet egg-yolks
on a sea of greys,
like turbulent and thrashing
thoroughbreds,
all straining at the reins,
before the gate flies open
and the beat of hooves,
like thunder,
shouts the heartbeat
of the race.

*****

I've grown so used to beauty
that it's now become
normality.

Is this a sin,
demanding that I beat myself
and shrink within my skin?

Can it be wrong to wear
a smile in my chair,
once more absorbed
in telly screen or monitor,
while sunset cries
for me to look
as it performs
extraordinary
leaps and reels
among the clouds outside?

There is no doubt
each moment is unique,
but it is also true
that this uniqueness
is not only found
in clichés of the sight,
so great that they demand
we give them all our beings
and leave behind the comfort
of our armchairs and our screens.

We mostly are content
to let the sun set by itself
and yet we still can find
a deeper joy
when we are caught, surprised
by beauty, much more shy
that grabs us without
spotlights, or the signposts
to some national park,
peacefully at home
with junk,
and semi-hid in dark.

For even in such places,
through the coughing and the dust,
a harmony survives
that moves the heart,
as ordinary things reveal
their real selves
and perfectly perform their part.

## ..and the winnerizzzzzzzzzzz...

The business of celebrity can drive me
mad enough to hurl
the telly out the window, which I'd do
if I were rich enough to buy a new one every day,
and not in fear that I might, prematurely,
freeze the thoughts of some poor passer-by,
whose mind might well concur with mine,
in loathing of the fame
that hangs around the necks
of human beings, whom chance has blest
to realise their strange desire
to soar above the rest.

Égalité, fraternité, are noble aims
that fit the state in which we all begin:
sulking upon our mother's breast,
as Mr Blake described our first attempt
to gain some comfort and security,
after our rude awaking with the clout
that shocked us into breath.

We enter nude, with no idea
of who we are, or what or where,
until we're told, or grasp
by instinct, the necessities
with which we can survive,
that suit us well enough
until the beast of competition
greens our eyes and gives our ears
its warnings that we might
get lost and buried in the masses,
like some undistinguished ant,
unless we climb upon a chair
or on the shoulders of our neighbours,
or their faces and their heads.

For life has limits and we must achieve
and shine, or else our lives
and all we've been and done,
will leave no trace behind when we are gone.

And this is, without doubt,
a fight we have to lose,
for in the giant scheme of things,
where universes sprout and die
more numberless than grains of sand
on all the beaches of the world,
the chance that our entire race
will be recalled by somebody
a million years from now,
is very slight, and odds are strong
that I and everyone I've met
will be no more than names
or faces on some unseen videos and snaps,
within a hundred years of our demise.

Yet still, while we survive,
we're driven to add glory to our names,
and try to gain some meaning to our life,
from things we've done and shaped:
our children and our friends,
and all those little things we change,
which must inevitably stay
a part of life's evolving way,
on which we stumble, blind,
as footprints proudly made
are quickly wiped away behind.

This truth holds good for all of us,
and none I think, is better
than another, in themselves.

Our bodies and our minds are driven
by the mix of genes and our environment
to make us how we are,
and  do the things we do.

And it is true we've always had among us, some,
whose names start off more known than the rest,
largely because their birth has given them

more power and more wealth,
while others have been known
for their force of arms, or brains,
which have delivered fame
and made them held aloft,
as inspiration, or a warning
to the mass of us, unknown,
except by family and friends.

But now, with so much leisure time
to spend before our screens,
or with our ears, locked into sounds
that may be heard by ears across the world,
we share the image of some person
who would be a millionaire,
or someone else who sings
a little better than the rest,
or those who strive to bake a better cake,
or be accepted for a job that they can only get
through sneers and putting down
the rest, who try to make it to the top,
where they will shine
as though transformed
from human into sun.

They stand there in a line
before some overpaid
and loud-mouthed idiot, who thinks
it is amusing to delay announcing the results,
by pausing long enough
for their cosmetic breath
to waft a dozen times around the hall,
while we await the ending of their words:
"the winner is................"
and desperately wish that some good god
would make this pregnant pause so infinite
that all this huff and puff might be the last
eruption from this misplaced arse.

I guess that there are many
who would slay, to take the place
of those contestants on the stage,
so they could smile nervously,
or weep, before the thousands who tune in
to wish them on, each week.

Perhaps they dream of how
amazing it would be
to be well-known wherever they may go;
to have a camera poke its lens
in every room of their existence
and transmit to all the world
the precious news that they have gained
their ticket to the hall of fame,
although it may be so
that love and hate will come to them,
just as it did before, but more, because
so many, jealously,
will yearn to share their fate

But will it bring more happiness
to be spread-eagled thus
before the lenses of the world,
where some of us
may know their names
and have some rough idea of who they are,
but actually are more concerned
with ordinary things,
that make the dramas of each life unique
without this crying need
to beat our chests and soar to peaks?

When they are filled with gas,
balloons are lovely in the sky,
as they compete to reach the top,
but just a little prick will make
each one of them go pop.

## Uncivil Service at the Tulle Préfecture

La fonctionnaire*has not been blest
with Aphrodite's visage
or a Playboy bunny's chest.

For any such distractions might impede
her serious transactions with the breed
of lowly beings who presume
to come before the desk
where she controls
by all the mighty laws of state
the life and fate
of all who have the nerve
to bring their nasty paperwork
before her tightly-buttoned vest.

Behind her desk she checks
each sub-clause of each document
for traps she can employ
to send them off to play
at  filling once again these forms
she will reject once more
when next they come her way.

How dare they think
she's only thereto serve
their need for forms endorsed
with her exalted name,
scrawled out in ink!

The nerve of it that they
should thus presume!
For she is more important, far,
than any president or TV star!

It's not her fault they grafted on
this strange half-human face,
before her body hit the earth
when last it rode through space.

*La fonctionnaire(de Tulle) is an apparatchik, notorious to all who seek to change a registration or a licence.

They'd told her she'd resemble
other members of the race
and dressed her in their style,
but they were not aware
that human eyes
might share some warmth,
and lips might smile.


## Keeping it dark

Wickeder than the witch of the West,
I keep my heart well-buttoned in my vest.
But my horns, which I often rasp and shave,
have a life of their own and refuse to behave.


## Here's A Marvel

Spiderman's nemesis:
"Funnel-web Head",
is no longer dead,
or so I have heard,
among other things,
from the beak
of the evil Robin
that stole the Batman's wings.

## Beep, Beep, Bloody Beep!

I am addicted to the news;
pursued around the house
by voices that resound
inside my mind,
to keep me constantly informed
of matters everywhere,
because I am a human being
and therefore have to care.

They ballyhoo so loud
that nasty bits of sound
can even stray within
the brick walls of the sanctuary
I've built to hide,
in hope to tiptoe in,
and meet my soul inside.

There is a constant clamour
in the background of my days,
until that moment comes
when I become aware
that I no longer hear
the sounds of life,
which truly can inspire me
with voices, so much sweeter,
that they bring to meet my ears.

And even in such times
when I have turned the volume off,
on TV and the radio, so I can be
in silence, only broken as I hear
the natural sounds, from my surrounds,
my mind won't give me rest,
but speculates on stuff
that's going on, somewhere
a thousand miles away,
and wallows in the stress
of wondering what it means
and what comes next.

Aye, strange it is that though
I'm wise enough to see
how useless are these thoughts
which so excite the being called 'me',
even this 'me' itself,
seems made from just such news,
and dreams of what will happen next,
that yet may never be.

So if I choose to shed it all
and throw it all away
that which remains
may be too different and rare
for me to recognise and read.

Then I may stare dumbfound and blind
confronted by the depths of unknown me
so dark, so deep, forever unexplored,
behind my mind.


## Bubble-Hubble

Bees in your bonnet
buzz buzz buzz.

What buzzing else
is brewing?

Spuds and meat
go burbling round
inside the Irish stewing,
reinforced with half a pint
of mother's ruing.

## London Encounter

He looked too huge
to be stuffed in a pram
on Guy Fawkes' night,
and was indeed the kind of guy
that might encourage you
to change your track
and risk the traffic, when your eyes,
being careful not to stare,
became alert that,
shambling up the pavement,
he was there.

His coat was far too large:
as if some pregnant sack of swag
was stuffed beneath,
or maybe poachers' pockets filled
the hugeness of his passage-blocking self.

And at its top,
you couldn't see much of the head that stuck
beyond the dark and shapeless coat,
above the fringe of Astrakhan
he'd surely snipped, in some secluded corner
of the Oxfam shop.

His baseball cap was pulled down low,
to leave a glimpse of blood-veined jowls
and conk, well-veined by fruits of many years
enjoyment of VP and other tonic
vintages, well-fortified with spirits
to promote illusions of rude health,
with rouge-like glow to keep at bay
the nosey interfering of some quack,
who might intrude into his life,
and ban the private pleasures
that gave meaning to his day.

Was he well-shaved? Well, what d'you think?
Though whether straying strands of grey
were sprouting from moustache, or beard,
or nasal passage-ways, was hard to say.

He made a stumbling progress
in ungainly boots, while from the space
between his hat and coat
emerged a strange cacophony of noise
somewhere between
an old tank-engine building steam,
and warming-up rehearsals
for the Black Dyke miners' band.

I could not help but gawp,
while crowded pavements emptied
as he loomed my way..........

Until too late to flee:
being foxed from crossing over
by the speeding cars, he had me trapped,
and grabbed my arm with iron grip
to wheeze into my face, "Excuse me sir,
I'm trying to raise some funds
for distressed gentlefolk,
for I, alas, am one."


## A London Seen

Playing Pooh
in London Zoo
is nowadays
the thing to do.

O see them come
from Shepherds' Bush
and Kensingbum,
where Nursey sits
by Piglet's stripy tum.

While Pooh
is very deep in Zen
and wisely humming
now and then.

## Take Note, Throat

Once it was really special:
every scoop that stuck
its lovely head
above the cornet's parapet
must be licked quick,
before the soggy end
began to drip.

The race with heat
competing with
the dare to bite;
the shriek
of nerves, freaked out
by freeze, to twang
like serpent fangs:
the masochistic price
of yumming into something
cold and lovely as an ice.

Of course the wise
and sensitive prefer to lick,
and still I do,
in graceful swoops,
unless I sit with tiny spoon,
to slip in genteel bits
between my dental wrecks, to slide
directly on the taste-buds,
bringing ecstasy
before the glide
down highways to the guts,
to chill my innermost inside.

In early days I was informed
that you could taste the whale in Walls,
and this perhaps was so,
although my tongue was not
fastidious enough to know,
despite the ease
with which it could discern
that Stork and butter
were as different as sand and snow..

And yet, when so-called 'parlours' opened
with Italian names,
and I first crossed the pond'
to greet the USA,
great mounds of real cream
informed me that there was, indeed,
a yawning gap between
the grease of whaley Walls
and such delicious gourmet feasts.

And then came sorbets, so refined
in fruity flavours, delicate,
that I could think
they'd really quench my thirst.

But how my taste buds lied!
For seconds after I'd
allowed these temptresses to slide
across the prudent
draw-bridge of the tongue,
I'd find myself assaulted
by outrageous thirst,
for something truly liquid,
to pour down the hatch, and calm
the shrivelling drought,
that brutally attacked my inner man,
and left me with
a hound-like, lolling tongue,
as though I'd travelled weeks,
on hands and knees, beneath
the mid-day, desert sun.

So there can be no doubt,
that though ice cream is really gratifying,
gulping down great glaciers of the stuff
is truly common-sense defying!

## Baghdad Nightrise

Far from the scent of flowers, yet rare,
I see the powers of darkness rise,
with beauty in their eyes,
through souks, that spread
their limbs between
the Tigris and the skies:

Like wings of moths,
that rise, to die
round lamps which blind
the eyes to stars,
with necklaces
of too much light.

So winds the purdah
of the night,
around Baghdad.


## In Tropic Climes

Here, in India, today,
the heat is kind
and bakes me
like a soufflé,
yet to rise

## Where Seekers Seek and Gurus Sit
*or "Mirror, Mirror on the Wall,
Who's the most Ego-less of All?"*

*Scene 1:*
When it comes to love and compassion
I welcome them all to my holy seat
and pour my grace on their needy heads
as they sing my name and touch my feet.

*Scene 2:*
What shall I wear for Satsang* today
to catch the guru's eye
so he can sense the beauty
of this non-existent "I"?

*Scene 3:*
As she fought to get to her space at the front
where she could touch the guru's feet
she found some unenlightened cow
had dumped her arse
on her special seat.

*Scene 4:*
My parents could not see
my real sacred self
and so I was chained to the name of Fred,
but now I'm Ananda Maya Das
I am so free
that all can see
my ego is completely dead.


*"Satsang" means literally "meeting in truth" but is usually the word for a meetings with guru or god.*

## On Indian Time

The clock stops here.
The minutes that chase me out of now
and drag me by the mind
towards the end
are lying now beside the path
and have become my friend.

No jobs, no school,
no bills to meet;
my movements, ruled
by rain or heat,
are walked with more respect
where bulls can toss their horns
as I edge round them
on the street,
and eyes examine ground
for potholes, or for rocks
that lie in wait
to jar my feet.

The movements of the clock
continue to record
the artificial gaps
which pass un-noticed
or extend like skies
which never set,
inside the open irises,
which fill my eyes.

## Houses of God

Houses of God
are often built
of brick or stone,
sometimes of skin,
and though the doors
seem sometimes locked
there always has to be
a loophole that is open,
in the hope that this
most honoured host
might choose to wander in.

So, sad it is, the welcome mat
has often turned to dust
before this unheard tread turns up,
and even then,
discovering the pews
are far too hard,
or fancy curlicues
too painful for the eye,
that's stung by scented air,
too filled with lies,
this precious guest
in his own house
will often yearn to get outside.

And thus he's like
to slam the door
and bolt off down the road
until he dives into that melting pot
of ecstasy and strife,
in which he's so uncomfortably at home,
in all this everywhere, called life.

## Hindu Temple

Walls of multi-coloured gods
and demons interlocked
and climbing for the sky,
with energy expressed through wild eyes
and hearts that pound and strain their chests,
while bodies writhe in acts of sex ,
that seem impossible to me
whose body was not made
to tie itself in knots
under some Yogi's scornful eye.

I'm carried by the crowd
to thread the lines of sadhus
with their begging bowls,
and shops that sell the plates,
already loaded with the offerings
of fruit and sweets,
composed for gods to eat,
but only with their eyes,
for none is gone, when plates
are handed back, still full
and newly cleansed with blessings
to be carried home and offered
to the family and friends.

Some paces further on,
with mighty forehead
white from vibhuti's\* sacred ash,
above his small, frustrated eyes,
the temple elephant is swaying
from foot to foot, to strain
the cruel limits of the chain
which holds him back
and makes him play
the same reluctant rôle each day,
before the throng of eyes that gaze.


\*vibhuti is ash from the burnt dung of sacred cows.

He reaches out his trunk
with nostrils open, held upright,
just like a beggar's palm
awaiting coins to backward pass
into his keeper's grip,
before he lays his trunk upon the heads
that bow, requesting blessings
from this living Ganesh, playing his part,
as keeper to the gates that lead
into the temple's heart.

Each day, at times prescribed,
he makes his ambling, tail-swishing way
around the shrines, until he finds
the idol, with a face just like his own, beside
the entrance to the hall,
where many deities reside,
and there he kneels as if in prayer,
then trumpets in the air
and bows three times,
just like the human beings
who worship at this shrine
before they dare to come before
the most exalted eyes
of those great gods who dwell inside.

They first go through a ritual
of beating on their foreheads
several times, before they cross
their arms across their chests
so that their hands, diagonalled, can grab
their earlobes, which they tug,
as legs, in harmony, bend knees,
to squat and rise three times,
as though they tried
to stretch their ears to such a size,
that Ganesh might mistake them for his kin
and give them all his love,
before he lets them in.

For now it's time to come inside
the darker, cooler halls
where feet are called to move in time
with wails and raucous yells
from out the nadaswaram\*as it fights
to win the race with muradungam's\* beat,
that rattles in the heads
of any gods who hope to sleep,
and make sure that their eyes are wide awake
to notice us arrive, as we come, shuffling in,
with plates of coconuts and fruits,
or banknotes held in fists, all packed together,
like a joined-up, living beast,
with many heads and hands.

We're funnelled in through clouds
of incense, choking in intensity
within the dark and stuffy space
where Brahmin priests
repeat their age-old rites
as servants of the ancient god,
whom they have bathed in ghee
and wrapped in finest cloth, that shows
how deep the pockets and the love
we're all prepared to give,
so all may know how great he is.

The priests receive the offerings, and wave
them several times before the gods
to offer them their chance to grab a treat or two
before returning them, now blessed
into the hands of those who wait
to take them home for all to taste.

And now the sacred moment comes,
with clanging bells and ancient chants;
the camphor is set fire on its plate
then offered round to each of us
who must receive with open hands,
to bathe our heads in these symbolic flames
that have a go at wiping
horrid karma from our brains.

\*Nadaswaram & Muradungam play S.Indian temple music.

And after sacred ash is wiped across our brows
the scarlet spot of cum-cum is applied
to that location claimed by Lobsang Rampa
to conceal the deep,
unopened wells of our third eyes.

And do we all believe
these deities with bright blue skin
and many arms, are truly here,
awake and listening?

Without a doubt, there's many do,
for where else would they find
such luxury, such food,
and such an endless line of fans?

Although philosophers may claim
their forms to be mere symbols for the truth,
the greater part of those who squeeze
through narrow entrances and fight to get a place
where they can stand for hours to wait
for that one moment when the gods
will open eyes and see them there,
are absolutely sure the gods they meet
are just as real as the film star,
whom they passed outside the temple gate,
whose giant portrait sprawls
across the walls and looms into the skies.

They pour into the street,
still shining, deep, in wonder,
that they've shared a space
with one so ancient and so wise,
who did not turn aside his face
when they entreated him for help
and laid their hearts before his feet,
for they are sure that he commands
a host of gods with powers so vast
that he can fill their future lives
with wealth and joy, and cleanse the slate
of all the sins that taint their past.

## Blue Mosque

Three feet above my head,
the massive chandeliers suspend
on iron chains, that almost disappear
into this emptiness, which seems
to soar for miles, to the inside of the dome,
where words in Arabic reveal themselves,
like waves that rise and fall across
the geometry of sky-filled stones.

This soaring inner skin
of some gigantic airship,
holds a presence, that amazes,
as I stand, or sit cross-leggèd,
with my head, unboundaried,
to welcome in, this force so tangible,
so powerful, and soft.

No wonder this religion will not tolerate
the image of a man or god within its walls!
No wonder that I'm called upon to wash
my parts and feet before I stiffly cross
my legs and take my seat!

The voice of the muezzin calls
from speakers high outside,
on minarets that pierce the sky;
but also here, inside this dome,
heaven itself is caught,
and held at home above my head.

While movements take my eyes to where
the bare feet of the faithful wander in
to pass through their repeated ritual,
prostrating to the force, that they believe
so fully in command

that they have little say
in how their lives will wend,
as they stand up and raise their hands
to heaven or fall down upon their knees,
to bend themselves,
face forward to the ground,
in full surrender to the emptiness,
they've found.

For me, who stands as witness here,
I am profoundly touched
that such a place could penetrate
the depths of my preoccupied
and unbelieving being, and mean so much.


### Song From A Minaret

Allah, in your eyes I am more naked
than the space between the stars.

Your hand is like a cloak of wool
as I stand trembling on the mountainside.

Your lips pour songs
of skylarks to my soul.

You fill my skin
with radiance, and I
am nothing but a space
within your skies
through which you shine,
as wine that pours,
with moonlight in its eyes.

## Going To Church

Forced in by school or family,
well-washed, and clothed in semi-best,
reluctantly I'd leave
the birdsong and the sky outside
and walk into the chill between the pews,
where half a dozen ladies in their hats
and half-reluctant husbands sat.

I'd put my bum down on the solid pew,
with centuries behind, of torturing
the backsides of communal ancestors
evicted from their household fires
to wail and chant.

Then down I'd go, to kneel with bended neck
and forehead leaning on my thumbs,
according to the rules I'd learnt
might best reward my labours
when troubling the almighty
for some little favours;
hoping that the special saintliness of me
might register before his eyes,
to halo me with light, or send
some thundering reply.

But sadly still unrecognised
by powers on high, I had no choice
except to carry on, and so I'd turn my eyes
upon the faded leather of the books
of hymns and common prayer,
to check this Sunday's fare
against the numbers on the board
and see if one that I enjoyed
were due this day for execution
by the choir of ancient dames
whose warbling trebles
could be counted on to climb
some feet above
the mumble of the blokes,
a demi-tone behind.

In front of me, beyond the hats,
the vicar's chant alerted me

that we already had set off
to some mysterious page inside
my pew-front library, I could not find,
until some neighbour warbler kindly
pawed my book and led my gaze
to fall upon the proper page,
but still I found it quite impossible
to keep up with the chase,
with all the leaps to bits
specifically designed to fit
this special day.

And then we moved into that part
which I refuse to speak
about "us miserable offenders"
with "no health in us",
For if he'd made us thus, it seems to me
he could have done a better job,
or born responsibility himself
instead of making us to miserably offend.

The rest of it is not so bad
as we wail back and forth
about the 'speed' or 'haste to help us',
as I wonder if the lord requires
this redundancy of prompts.
Perhaps he's wearing ear-plugs
in defence, and did not hear,
so 'haste' must double-up with 'speed'
if he's to helter down from Paradise,
to answer all our needs.

We then continue to some readings
and a sermon, while I make
a study of the flies, that whirl or crawl
across the well-stained-glass
whose solid-coloured shapes
they may mistake for garden plants,
more interesting for foraging, than hairs
in ancient nostrils, snoring in and out,
ecclesiastic airs

We treble through some hymns
where I select the lines I choose to sing
and those which I refuse,
until I'm forced to grovel in my pocket
for the pennies I must drop
into the velvet hat, which waits,
too patiently, before my face.

And once it goes up to the front
for counting of the loot,
there starts a shuffling and a squeezing past,
as from the pews emerge
the ladies in their hats, and spouses,
gaunt, along with some
unpleasantly cherubic, young
and spotty persons, near my age,
who join the ragged line, that moves
toward the wafers and the wine,
while I, the unconfirmed
am, mercifully, allowed outside.

Once thus released, I breathe
the grassy air, refreshed by rain,
and mooch about the graveyard, or enjoy
a celebratory fag behind the wall, until
the door swings open and the vicar stands
strategically upon the steps,
to greet in person every sheep
among his flock who'd kept awake
for long enough to offer up
their hands to shake,
and ferret out some warm,
appreciative word
about the bits of sermon that they heard.

I wander through the graveyard,
where old ghosts still yawn
a protest through their toothless mouths
at this disruption to their peace,
as they give thanks to Him, up there,
it only happens once a week.

## Without The Holy Clothes

Each rock, each tree, I meet,
speaks for itself, and all its ancestry,
without the cloying
dream of some created deity,
to fudge and blunt its
simple truth of being.

The clarity through which I walk
is new to me and free
of that distracting junk
which so much lumbered
up my brain.

I meet each self
as perfect as my mind
can let it be
and that is quite
enough for me.


## Settling In The School By The Fields

Do they feel too: these flowers?
Petals shifting colours,
stroked by rippling bodies
of the bees, buzzing beneath
the heart of sun, which swims among
the quiet clouds and trees.

Somehow their leaves cast shadows
on the flesh beneath my skin
so freckled is the day
in transience of light and shade.

And then I meet a pair of eyes
that have no darkness, only
the open smile of peace,
as evening drifts around my soul,
inside this breeze, where all
I thought myself, is lost
and all that's left is dancing leaves.

## L'Église de St Sylvain

This church is small and strangely shaped,
with transept longer than its nave
and just as wide.

It makes a comfortable cross,
with foot end shorter than its arms
proportioned in a form which satisfies:
each limb being wide enough,
to make me feel unstretched:
as though I sit within a living room,
with space for comfy chairs and fireplace
to shelter me from night and gloom.

Whatever chance, or careful hands,
have given me this harmony,
I cannot say, nor can I tell its age
and this is rare for me,
who loves to see
the stolid Romanesque
or set my eyesight free
to climb up high
where gothic arches turn to spires
that pierce a way
to heaven, through the sky.

Those stones whose shape
might give me clues
to guess the date
when first those well-trained hands
inserted them in place
are stolen from my mind
by my surprise, that smiles
as my eyes grow wide

To see that all the light
that flows in from the skies
is tamed, by windows void of arches
framed in solid, rectangles of stone
which makes it feel
quite unlike a church,
and more like home

They turn me from a stranger to a friend
who's just dropped in to share a cup of tea
with some old god, who's warm and kind
and not that angry, bossy fool
who often comes to mind.

## Dry Haiku

A flower dying
in pain, praying for thunder,
thirsting for rain

## Wet Haiku

Out of the tumult
of the skies gentle water
falling on my eyes

## A Biblical View

The ark rides
the boundless ocean,
over the swirling tides
of fish and crustaceans,
in billions.

While Noah
fishes with pride,
knowing that he's
the one who's helped
his chosen
'two-by-two's
survive.

*This next poem has hopefully found
its perfect form, after starring,
imperfect, in 2 earlier books:*

## Inside Stained Glass

In the cathedral, grey and high,
adrift in incense , floating by
the effigies of saints, the light,
through stained-glass windows,
flutters on the deacon's fat behind,
while a class of sixth-form
schoolgirls fills his mind.

Look up and up: the great, square stones
grow thinner, as they narrow to a stop,
where correlated arches spring,
like sinewed branches, meeting
at the point of praying fingers,
lost a thousand years,
before intrusive floodlights marred
their stretching arrow's flight
to pierce the mystery of God.

Down on my knees, the hands of Christ
caress my head, and deep
within my fontanel, I feel them unknot
the stress and pain,
to unlace all that's left of me,
and darkness melts to colours
while the breath
is gardened with such scents, that I
am totally unfenced,
to merge into the sunset sky
and nothing more is left for me
to do, or be.

But in my ears the music dies,
and voices, seventeen years old,
in perfume, drifting by,
blow wide my eyes, and I
have elbows on the praying shelf.

The stone is cold, and currents in the air
raise gooseflesh as I stare,
with new-found angel eyes,
into the eyes of her,
beneath the wild red hair
with miniskirt above her thighs.

The saints are all asleep.
They lie like that all night
with no temptation there,
within the gates they close at eight o'clock.

But I
am shut outside.


## What Is Masochism?

Life without a moon
shining on spires
like this


## Bright Night Alleyway

Dressed in silver, whispering,
the junkyard cat
unwraps
the chicken bones
by moonlight.
Picks his teeth with stars.

*Some Shakespearean beginnings, start with:*

"A poor player who struts and frets his hour
upon the stage, and then is heard no more."

These were the words that Shakespeare gave Macbeth,
while Dr Donne made mockery of Death,
believing, with such faith, in afterlife,
that he was sure that Death himself would die.

And where am I, beyond three score and ten,
as time is closing in and my ambitions narrow down
to hopes for peaceful days,
when I at last have stashed away the toys,
that clamour still to gobble up my time,
and still succeed in making me believe
that anything I do can be of some significance
for those, who come behind,
in all that endless tail that disappears,
where beings, still unborn, perhaps may be
deflected by some energy, that I've
been pushed to loose, by forces that took life
a billion years before my own.

It's strange and possible that you may also wonder
why it is I see the beings of the future as my tail,
not my spew; or breath, I blow before me as I go.

And yet it's not so strange; for my excreta,
like my falling hair, my layers of skin,
and teeth, I left behind for fairies,
will survive, transformed to useful stuff
when every memory of me has blown away in winds,
like these, my body leaves behind.

And thus before is not before, behind is not behind,
and this, perhaps, is one brief insight into Time.

For when I try to leave this stage I find no door,
nor any place to go,
for time is always here, inside this mind,
which makes believe these strange ideas
of 'now' and 'then' are so.

## Ingredients for Mr Shakespeare's Recipe

"What a piece of work is man!"
Indeed it often can
bewilder me
when I confronted am
by this extraordinary yoking
of profundity and ham.

My very mind is boggled as it tries
to understand this ballroom
made of meat, where atoms dance
combining out of wisdom
or from chance
to make these strange
unwieldy objects rock and roll
around that stranger music
they call 'soul'.

Some clever folks
have posed the question:
'What comes first,
the body or the mind?'
Or even more:
how can it be
that our solidity
is on the whole
constructed out of atoms
which themselves
are largely holes.

Such questions
rise and fall,
with little fruit to eat
while man limps onward
in his hope
to so adjust
the moment he must meet,
that he might make
a change that will survive
"as long as men may live
and lips may speak".

## No Pain In The Stain

"Out damnèd spot!"
In days gone by, methinks
it was a problem which was found
most often in that odd and strange accessory,
that's called 'a tie',
which seemed to be designed
specifically for eggy stains,
with chevron end, to be well-dipped in soup or tea
by every leather-elbowed intellectual
or pedagogue, and therefore was the sign
of thoughts, profound, that shone in such a mind.

And there were products
that were made specifically
to lift old egg or gravy from the cloth
which went all shelvy, then could be brushed off
only to leave a faded bit behind.

But now my neck no longer is enlivened
by these rags, so carefully selected to display
my personality, my clothes are far more
practical and down to earth.

And yet the damnèd spots will still arrive,
when knees go down to ground to seek
for things I need amidst the subterranean
darkness of the lower shelves,
or grope among my flower beds for cunning weeds,
only to rise with something horrid
clinging to the knees.

And as for laps:
they clearly are created to display
whatever diet passed my lips that day,
propelled by clumsy hands or elbows
that have found some way
to leave a greasy sample on my front
that's cunningly passed by
the feeble paper napkin, if it still is there,
and not on the floor beneath my chair.

The Devil has endowed me
with such clumsiness that I must wear
such spots and blodges, like a toad,
well splattered from the trucks
that blunder through the mud
and puddles on the road.

And thus it is a blessing
I have shed all hope
of luring lovely creatures
with the beauty of my form,
to share my bed and home,
and now I'm unashamed to be
just what remains of me,
resigned to smile or sometimes grieve,
for life has left few aces up my sleeve.

Such damnèd spots are mine
however much I duck.
The wheel that spatters mud,
has been ordained to spray,
whatever patterns on my being
are on the menu for the day.

## The Way Of Untruth

The ages on me lie,
for truth is shy
to be a body or a face.

The masks I wear
have not the strength
to lock me in their place
and manifest me there,
or anywhere.

For I am stripped more bare
than nakedness.
and nakedness is still
too many clothes to wear.

## Clocking In And Out

"My time is out of joint".
At least, it seems to be,
and this is doubly so, where clocks defy
our true location on the earth,
revolving in its journey,
which reveals sun and stars,
appearing to our East
before our travelling eyes,
which harbour the belief
that they are rising
through the skies.

For time here is distorted
by the whims of politicians
who've decreed our time must be
the same as that of nations
spread so distant to the East
they see the sun a real
hour or two ahead of us.

And in the summer one more hour
is stolen from our clock,
so, as the season wanes, we're forced
to rise in deepest night,
while at the other end, the sunset
lingers on, while we are still engaged
in washing up the dinner plates.

I guess it has advantages
to have our time so far awry
for if we followed real time
the disappearing stars
and beauty of the dawn
would rarely meet our eyes.

But still I'd rather rise, without the need
for artificial light and dawning cold
to threaten my stiff limbs with frost
when I must climb from bed
to make my creaking way downstairs
to answer nature's morning call.

But that is not the story's end: no, not at all,
for I no longer am a wage-slave in the thrall
of my alarm clock's horrid din,
that's worse than clashing bins
at drowning out my neighbour
cock-a-doodle's morning hymn.
I have the choice to jettison my clocks
or turn them to the wall and thus
adjust my time to suit my needs,
and anyway, what is this thing of ticks and tocks
beyond the changes in the sky
that raise or dim the light that meets my eye?

My consciousness can take a moment
and extend it to infinity,
or so it seemed on LSD,
and if not so extreme
it certainly can be extended to a length
that's scarcely bearable,
when I am stuck and pinned
like Eliot in some soirée,
or never-ending lecture,
with an audience so small
it gives me prominence, as I am fidgeting,
and battling with my yawns.

And when in ecstasy,
time yanks me from my seat
and opens wide my eyes
to life's mad, roller-coaster ride,
of wonder fear and joy,
how fast it flies when I would
grab its legs with heart and hands
imploring that it stay!

And this grows urgent now
as Father Time comes closer
with his sharpened scythe and deep desire,
to slice me into bits which soon enough
will wriggle off as worms
or blaze and roast in fire.

## Pills for Ills

Each day I break my fast with pills
designed to keep me still alive
some years and months beyond the span,
allotted by the Gods to man.

I really want to do with less,
for side effects must come
from all the junk in some,
and they are hardly natural foods
my forebears might have tilled, or raised,
though even these are suspect now,
of poisoning by sprays, or made
of chemicals as numerous as these small pills,
I harvest from the pharmacy.

It clearly is the case, however
I may strive to be a 'new age' man,
imbibing and consuming only stuff
that's made organically,
it's doubtful it will make
much difference to this
carcass, full of colourings
and additives, which often wants
its food too fast, or lusts with greed
for flavours which excite the taste-buds
more than wholemeal bran or seed.

Perhaps I could cram in enough
of just such healthy goodies
to extend my life some weeks
or even months, but still
I am too late to bolt the door.

The horse already gallops off the track
and since some pills were hidden in his oats,
I guess he'll blindly carry on,
going round and round,
as one by one, the parts of him
give up the ghost
until what's left gets turned to smoke,
or buried in the ground.

## Knock Knock

And shall I die
and not come back?

No shadow on the doorstep,
and no silhouette on pane;
at fingertips, no movement
as the glass stands dumb and clear,
while ouija board won't rise
above the knees,
for knock knock, no-one's there.

I've gone so very far inside
that nothing's left alive
inside this skin.

There's only the merest trace of a soul
that seems to be waving bye-bye
as it whizzes off, struggling,
down the black hole.

And now there is only
this comforting sound:
"Atissue, atissue, we all fall down!"


## Momentarily

At every time, I am reborn.
The man who has stood
is gone.

## Memoir To Myself

I have become, too much, a wise old fool,
who comments on a world
that he has largely left behind,
engaging with each line
to try to find some wit,
or words that fight a combat with themselves
to spark, original and new,
a fire, that might revive this tepid stew.

Must I accept this slow decay
that roots me to an armchair or a screen,
when sun comes up
announced by birdsongs to display
the music and the colours of a day
that once would yank me from my seat
and send me out to breathe on hillside paths,
through windy trees.

Most carefully, I've bound myself
with walls, well-coloured
with some paint that is my own,
and hung on them some pictures that I love,
among the photos of a life
that once was mine.

So I may smile now and then,
as I pass by and know,
unless catastrophe decides
to shake my safety to the core,
I am secure.

And thus I can reside inside my shell
with little need to go outside
and risk whatever life's unruly tide
might wash along to pour into my mouth
that rather hopes to open now, to sing a song,
or drink whatever essence
might convince me I am young.

I've seen so much, that I
no longer seek for novelties,
or eyes, that might disturb the heart
which is a threat if it decides
to beat with too much speed.

Indeed, my worn out knees
and shallowness of breath, decree
that if I move too fast,
I may be rushing to my death.

But if to be alive means nothing more
than shoring up my walls
and stopping gaps where drafts come in
what is the point of that?
And when the world is only seen
through double glaze
it might as well be bars
that frame my gaze.

Perhaps I fool myself in bumbling
round my garden with the bees,
to find delight in seeing seeds
I've planted, fight their way to light
and show me who they are,
reminding me I play some part
in offering some corner of my days
to that long journey
born in gas and fire to become
a planet filled with life and song.

Indeed such moments smile
on my time, so I will quite forget
all other things when I am busy
with some plant or wondering
what kind of bird it is
that can so sweetly sing.

But even so, my garden has a wall
that can't keep out a universe
whose cries of agony can drown
the quiet burble
of the stream of life
when ears like mine are
tuned to hear such cries,
which call my limbs
to oil themselves to be of use,
for distance from such scenes
is no excuse.

And so, I send out messages
which flow to those who nod
because they are my 'friends'
and will agree, while still
the helpless drown beneath the sea
and all of us are slowly sucked,
by sickness and old age, to disability.

What can I do,
where all these thoughts rebound
to echo round my skull, except
to turn the volume down,
to pause and breathe and look around
at life which still goes trotting by,
so easy and so used
to pains and happiness
which rise and fall in their own
natural tides?

They touch this place
where I remain as I have always been:
the unclothed being inside, unchanged ,
and still a new born babe
with eyes unjaded by
the passage through this life
and so much more,
that tails on behind
and looms before.

The only place that I can be
is where I am
with eyes still sometimes wide,
enough, to tell my mind
I can get by, as I go step by step
to meet whatever is to come.

I'm suddenly aware,
that every thing
that ever was,
walks with me here,
where it's impossible for me
to be alone.


## What's New?

The whole world does what it does
while I don't have
to move an inch.

There is no-one I need to meet,
and not a place
where I must go.

This 'freedom' is a word
that people use,
as if they knew.

But I can only say
that there is nothing
that I know or have to do.


## The Joker Speaks

I am only the fool.
I know I am worth nothing.
So what can I lose?

## Here Be Tonics For Electronics

Screens are now my life:
all day they flash and grin
and try with great success
to lure me in.

They often come
with extra catch
of voice attached
which natters on
whatever I am doing;
and thus I do
with only half an ear
tuned in. But still
they seem to sap my energy
like leeches hardly felt,
or bowels filled
with gut-worms chewing.

All at once, some moment
wipes the windows of my head
and I look out surprised
to wonder what has happened
to the hours that have fled,
with all that information
that I have not really heard
when I was trying to think
while only up to taking in
a fraction of the world
that is my life,
being hacked away
as every tick and tock
moves closer to
the ending of my day.

So why not switch off all the screens
and curl up with this book
that calls to me to spend a while
with characters and plot
revealing as I look
their depth and style?

Because it's so much easier
to peer at text, unrolling on the screen
than tax my eyes in trying
to disentangle print
that's hard to read,
as cataracts like frost
obscure my sight
and drag away the clarity
that used to be
the boundary of my life.

As soon as I descend the stairs,
half-headached from the strain
of e-book flashing on my brain,
another screen goes on, to view
my inbox and my Facebook
while I read the online Guardian
to double up the news,
which chatters from my radio,
as I consume my muesli
and my feast of pills, designed to stretch
my time on Earth, despite my ills.

And thus I'm like to carry on
whenever I return
from sorties to the outside world
for shops and gardening
until the time to cook
my evening meal arrives, accompanied,
by radio, until I settle down
before  the evening's telly: my reward
for all the strenuous work I've done.

There have been many times in my long life
when I was years away from screens,
except the rare and treasured
sortie to the flicks,
and looking back it seems
that I perhaps was happier then,
just living in the world,
allowed to be with ordinary dreams.

My senses then seemed more alive
and I believe they still might push aside
the speakers and the screens
to raise me from the semi-dead
revived and blossoming, to meet
each moment, as it wanders in,
content to be its own unique and special thing.
If only I would switch the music off, and sing!


## Close to the Home of Friends

The houses huddle close,
with fingers to their lips,
to hush the urge
to crash the peace
with one astonished "Wow!"
at such a beauty
as I stumble down the path
into their privacy.

Their whispers stop
and wait for my departure,
as I stand,
dumbfounded by silence,
as I harvest all the ripeness
of the colours and the trees
that scent the air and justify
their comfortable ease.

For thus they feed, hospitably,
this traveller, who appears,
for this brief moment in their scene,
to give them cause
to share some pithy thoughts,
to seed their conversation,
once this eavesdropper has breathed,
then gone elsewhere.

## In An Alaskan Cabin

Awakening, I take
great bites of silence,
as I lift the mask
from off my eyes,
to let the all-night
daylight enter in.

Amazing that this audience
of glaciers and pines
still waits outside,
and all I have to do
to share their skies
is open up this door,
and take a step
with one gigantic breath
and two enormous eyes.


## Nome Pomes

*There's no place Like Nome (Alaska),
where you'll meet:*

### Helen Of Nome:

Is this the face that munched a thousand chips?

*And her place, which is, of course, a*

### Nome-Home:

Just another pile
of useful junk,
but more
lived in.

## Where Patients Learn Patience

Appointed to meet le medécin
at half-past nine, I come on time,
in hope to find an empty room
where I may read back issues
of Équipe or Paris Match, to stretch
my linguistic skills
for half an hour or so, while
comfortably ensconced and waiting for
the doctor's door to open up.

But then I meet the first blow to my hopes,
as I walk in with muttered
"bonjour, messieurs, dames,"
to find three seats already filled
with anything but cheer,
as every face seems stocked with care
and lost in contemplation of deep ills,
distracted only by the hope
that small increases in the volume
of the chat beyond the door,
may be the signal that it soon
will open to that special room.

But still it stays tight shut,
as eyes with their extinguished hopes
examine one more time the movements
of their watch's hands, as if their irises
might push them on towards that moment,
when the door will open to reveal
the ritual shaking of the hand,
as Dr Danielle lets out her last
embarrassed visitor,
who mumbles to the door,
self-consciously concealed
behind the eyes, which fear to meet
those of the waiting customers
who tap their anxious feet.

She calls a name, and one, who's waited
just two hours, leaps up, in release,
as if he'd left the plague he brought
beneath the poorly-cushioned seat.

Her hand extends to give the ritual shake
and he is welcomed to her den, to give
his 'Carte Vitale', his symptoms and his cash,
between the medical catastrophes
with which the telephone intrudes,
while he is growing steadily more scared
of being devoured alive
by all the waiting customers,
who surely now have mounted up,
at least to twenty-five.

Out there, the paranoia rises
as each victim of some dire,
contagious malady, comes shuffling in,
after the "bonjour messieurs, dames,"
to wedge their panic in between
outrageous coughs and sneezes,
clenching guts as best they can,
before they rush, in hope
of some relief, into the smallest room,
only to re-emerge, after the public sound
of a flush, well purged, perhaps,
but unrelieved of gloom.

We peer at one another, wondering
who'll be the first to croak, perhaps,
or at the least to "hrumph!"
impatient, from their seat,
in hope the drop-outs might permit
the chance to scale the queue
enough to let us home
before the lunch grows cold,
or get us back in time to meet
the meter reader, who is due
between the hours of twelve and two.

There's even some blasé enough
to slide down to their necks
and start to snore,
but that's not me, for I am still
in terror that I might drop dead
before next week, unless
I get my troubled flesh
inside that door.

## Being Supernaturally Yours

They say that ghosts aren't real,
those grown-ups,
so sure they're right.

But I am thronged,
each way I look,
by spirits in the air,
they cannot see, or feel, because
their senses have been blinded, so
they do not know
that they are watched.

Why don't they fear
this sudden coldness that appears?
How can they wander through
the darkening woods and be so unaware
of corpses hanging from the trees?

How can they sleep and never hear
the creaking of the board, where feet
that never rang the doorbell
tiptoe through the hall,
to try again to find
the bedroom where I sleep,
in terror they will enter through the wall,
whatever care I take to lock my door?

And even as I stand with key in hand,
I cannot turn it, for I know
that when they come
to freeze my blood and stand my hair
on end, I'll need to run,
to safely squeeze between my mum
and dad, so huge and warm,
and smelly in their sheets.

If only I were sure
they'd let me in....

And how they laugh,
each time I flush the loo,
with door already open
for my rush
in terror through the house,
as Captain Hook
comes claw-first from the
bog, to rip me into shreds...

I'm really not afraid of spiders
in the bath, for they may be enticed
to climb on rolled up newspapers
and carted out at speed
before they can escape
to web my head and suck
the juices from my veins.

But when I'm deep immersed
in grey and cooling suds,
the branches, in the darkness,
tap upon the window, like
the skinless knuckles of a ghost
and so I cower by the hour,
till I dare to brave the chilly air
and run back to the safety of my room
where I can grab my cowboy hat,
my gun, and wooden sword,
to keep them all at bay,
while mummy, smiling,
thinks I only play.

If only she would know
the horrid dangers,
lurking round her life
she'd have at hand more weapons
than her rolling pin, her frying pan
and onion-peeling knife.

## I Wandered Lonely As A Car

I need some help from Wordsworth to convey
these roadsides now: which drive away
all thought, as they invade my being,
to make me only eyes,
without the words to dive
enough within, to truly swim
among such colours, and such forms,
that I may pour in other glasses
some small essence of this sight,
and how it drenches me,
beyond the usual similes
to other forms and light.

Compared to this
a field of daffodils,
that dances on a windy day,
beside a lake,
is easy to express...

For here my sight is soaked
in tones and subtleties,
that crowd this road's descent
through passing mists
and passageways of sun
that light the dew,
that soaks the leaves of ferns
and bows their heads
to show their backs,
aflame with brown, so pure,
it seems the essence of itself.

All down the edges of the road,
they contrast with the grass,
all shiny from its morning bath.

While framing every curve,
cascades of multi-coloured leaves
unwreathe themselves, to stream
through mist and rays of sun
in harmony of colours
like a palette of experiments
from yellow through deep red
to darkest brown.

Each leaf is separate,
and moves in individual breeze,
to make a social symphony
that human beings
have not yet achieved,
and each of them is clothed
in its most lovely dress,
astonishing our eyes,
as it gets ready to let go
and flutter down to death.

I am not there, as I inscribe
these lines, inadequate
to bring across the wonder
that I met, but even
as I rode I started to reflect
on their approach to leaving life,
so different from ours.

However hard we try
to sparkle in our final hours
we are reduced by modern
medicine and fears,
to creep towards our ends
in hospitals or homes,
where we have little chance
to rise up from our beds and dance.

I guess it's foolish to complain.
"The good die young", the cliché says,
and it is clear that smitten down
by accident or war, we may pass on
aflame, or coloured by
the brightest blood, to horrify
and fright our witnesses, and yet,
the minds borne off, perhaps,
exactly at, the perfect time,
may well approach their end like leaves
that start their change to skeletons and dust
while still afloat and dancing in the breeze.

They make a test for me, more hard
than I have faced at any moment of my life:
to take this stomach stuffed with medicines,
and mind that wriggles back to memories
and fears of what's to come,
and shrug them to the side, so I
may have a real try to leap out of my seat
and take my feet to any road
where I may hang my thumb
and welcome all that life may bring along
until it smites me down
while I'm still spinning
in my dance.

I'd like to end
like Chaplin stuck inside a drum
when Limelight ended and
his day was done.*

---

*\* In the film, 'Limelight', Charlie Chaplin, playing an old comedian, falls off stage and gets stuck in a drum, which the audience thinks is part of his act, but he's dying, as he watches the love of his life, as she dances on the stage.*

## The Teaching of Leaves

Ambushed by dancing leaves,
*aflame on eddies in the breeze,*
my being seems to ride
so high above my eyes,
no camera could catch the ecstasy
that nudes my heart
to totally embrace
each different shape of leaf,
that bears itself, so joyfully
unleashed and free.

My being is tugged and I am led
to far beyond the fields
of birth and death,
to meet the source of breath,
which falls and rises
to a beat that is alone its own
where measurements of time
remain unknown.

And all the miracles of now
forever stay completely free
of all the tyranny of words
that snatch it from the ecstasy
of dancing with itself
and violate its unity. like swords
which hack it into bits
and tell each bit to know itself
as separate and die.

For this is mind's most cruel crime
to cut us from our real selves
then lock us up in time.

## Where All Paths Meet

Letting go of everything,
at last I find the lake
where the moon likes to sleep
when it's awake.

## Horses

Horses, still ...
now very still,
beside the railway,
no longer
charge away,
now steam
has long become
a legend told
by ancient steeds,
that's only whinnied
down the years,
from mare to foal,
in tales,
that seem
like myths,
passed down from
mouth to mouth
out of
the oaty mists
of dream.

## Train Faces

Because the seats that face the front are full
I find myself unique, inside this train,
as I am forced to sit
where back and rump precede my brain
and eyes must be confused
for what's before must be behind.

But why should this seem strange
for past and future cannot help
but be united in my mind?

But let me not digress
to philosophic thoughts, but simply stare
across the molecules of air
into the secret faces worn by English folk,
reserved and fortified,
safe from the stares of eyes
that are so much a part of life
where I sit down to drink a chai,
before my battle for a place
inside a bus, where half the passengers
are forced to climb up on the roof
or hang outside.

I don't know what they make of me,
or if they even see that I am there
as I am merged into this ordinary journey
for their lives,
to be forgotten
faster than the glance
which gave me access to those eyes
which bravely hide
the terrors and adventures
of their country lives.

## Soller to Palma Train, 1980

Dark train:
night faces gaze
through glass,
at trees, strong, green,
and dripping rain.

Aromas of the pines
that seep in
to revive
dull nostrils, pass
through creaking steel
and rattling glass.

Dark train:
bears flesh and bone,
careening on the rails,
clinging live,
above the precipice,
until the points that switch
us through the fields
of rocks and thistles,
hungry goats and sheep.

Dark train:
inspires poems,
where flashes fly
and crackle
from the lines above the track,
to flash the faces:
white as dust,
and bits of leaf,
outside, are driven back
in cyclones to the sky
by shrieking gales that sweep
above the teeth
that crowd the jagged summits
of the waves beneath.

### Deya, Majorca

Fiesta of exiles.
Bar in giant rockery;
avalanche of rain on rooftop,
white claws rising from the sea;
roses and pines silent outside.


### As Time Goes By

By the lake:
a distance from
the falling minutes;
trees span centuries
above the boats,
that carry through the darkness
voices on the waves
that disappear...


### Under Mulhaçen*

Like a sieve
through which
a garden sends
its scents at sunset,
in Granada,
I am lost again:
under Mulhaçen*:
a voice crying;
a guitar;
river winding its way
under the stars.


*Highest peak in Spain, close to Granada*

## The Last Haiku Master*

The old poet finds
his ink and brushes,
hung with frost
but still alive.

He sees the vapour of their breath
wind up into the sky
and climbs it with his sight,
in hope he may surprise
some petals dancing
round the trees...

but meets there
only wind, that bites
with whetted teeth
and freezes up those eyes,
whose love for life
has kept them young
so many years.

He shivers, as it shrieks,
while underneath he hears
his own voice nagging, deep,
inside his ears:

"Already May,
but branches still
are black against the sky,
and hung with ice!

What is this act I've done?

I fought with such delight
to catch the being of the sun
so I could hold him totally,
within my lines.

*whose story first entered my life 46 years ago,
and he still isn't sure that I, his lowliest son,
am quite the one, to tell it right.

If I can't find a way
to set him free,
all living things will die
because of me."

He takes down every haiku
from his walls,
then scoops them up in armfuls,
till his shirt is stuffed
and he can feel each leaf,
that flutters, still alive,
against his heart,
as from his knees
he gathers all his life
and staggers up.

With muscles
straining with the weight
of paper that he bears,
he climbs the mountain path
until he finds
a shelf, as high as sky,
where he can lay his burden down.

He stands, as best he can,
in fragile silhouette, before
the fragments of the stars,
between the clouds,
torn by the wind to shreds
like ancient shrouds.

He crouches,
low behind a rock,
and strikes a fire
which he shelters
with his hands,
and in its light
he catches sight
of haiku that he loves:

Each one of them, a moment
seized from time
and perfectly recorded
in three lines,
that made their way from nowhere
to inspire his mind.

With dignity he bows to them
and says his last goodbye,
and then lies down
among these dearest friends,
as fire makes them one
great beacon, calling out
to life, to come.

The children stare in wonder
as the light mounts up
and reaches out long arms
between the trees.

They race out with delight
to catch the petals
dancing on the breeze.

## Chinese Masterpiece

Some characters made
by strands of ink,
convey a truth
I cannot think.

## Insight

What an idea:
to simply be here!
I think I'll give it a go.

As soon as I find myself here,
I'll let me know.

## Letting Things Wait

Deep sleep,
sheep of the deep,
I'm snuggled in wool
and warm and full,
while the days disappear
with no me here.

## Frogs

To celebrate the beauty of the moon,
the frogs have made
gigantic caves inside their chests,
where drums and brass compete
with echoes of themselves to croak
in one great voice
their yearning serenade.

The thunder of their song
vibrates inside my dream
to hurl my mind awake
with startled eyes.
that think the dawn has come.

But I have been deceived
because this light is far too pale
that parts the drapes of night
to peer inside my room with quiet face
and check that I'm alright.

Perhaps it's her silver heart that gives
the lovelorn frogs the beat
that makes their music sink and rise,
as I drift back to happy dreams,
where planets dance behind my eyes.

## Wake Up In The Morning Poem

When cloudy curtains part,
the sunset and the dawn compete
for which of them can touch my heart,
and multiply its beat.

The dawn here has the better chance,
because it's rare, that its soft light
can find a gap between my drapes,
so placed, that it can warm my eyes
and bathe my face.

Though sometimes
it will ambush me,
as I come stumbling home
from some last curtain call,
or very late last-stand,
from which I tip-toed down the stairs,
with shoes in hand.

It's rare that I will hear it come,
for frogs and crickets sing
with voice enough to hide its tread,
and drops of dew are silent as they land
on blades of grass,
though sometimes they awake
my nostrils for a sniff
that's long and deep,
with scents of life, renewed,
as I fall back to sleep.

Its skies don't dramatise with shades
as wild as sunset, with its paint,
that's splashed on stretched-out clouds,
of every hue, that's born in fire,
from shyness in embarrassed pink
to mad desire.

But eyes have grown used
to see the drama of this show,
and though the heart can race
to photograph this scene,

it lacks the quiet touch,
or peeping patch of light
that shyly takes our hand
and pulls us out to meet
the new-born sun,
when it comes out
to wake the land.

And thus while crowds
are dazzled by
the sunset colours,
which must surely win,
dawn, on its quiet horse, trots in...

And then the birds of day,
who seldom raised
their voices until then,
will, all at once,
wake up and sing.


### How It Was

To wake-up
in make-up
is a fright.

For morning
seems to dawn
deep in the night,

because the hand
forgot to click
the button
on the bedside light,

and yesterday's
fag-end drags on,
unlipped,
but lipsticked,
in the night.

## Where's The Happy Ending?

My world's all shaken up.
The march of day to day
halts in some god-forsaken spot,
as if there hung
some light that turned from green to red
and skipped the amber of the sun.

Am I the only one
who's started counting down the days
as though Death's yawning maw
were just a couple of fields away?

We loved the speeding up and down,
with all its fairground song;
of hurdy-gurdy rides,
as round we swung, on perches
that seemed safe, until
the tremors came along,
to shake us side to side
and tangle up our wires
till we jammed up, eye to eye,
with threats that we will die,
all strangled up, like insects lost
in some unsolvable, unfinished game
where we are asked to find
the ending of a line that started safe
and clear, outside.

I did not ask to be created at this time,
but long ago, I ceased the fight
for different light and let my heart
perform the part, dictated by the beat
of other feet, and fair enough,
it thrilled, or fell asleep,

with aches, or smiles as its treats,
or blows were meted out, according to my fate,
well-hidden in some box,
to which I had no key.

Such is the lot of many beings like me.
So is it just my age, and special fate
that make me feel the land beneath my feet
is being gobbled by the sea,
and neon signs are closing round
the safety of my plot,
with shouts and screams,
through jagged teeth,
that eat my dreams
and gnaw to dust
the walls of my retreat?

I used to have a mind
that could effectively turn off
such scenes, but now I can no longer
fit inside its frame,
the fire-door, that once
would keep me cool and dry.
 .
There is no way that I can ban
the clouds that fill my sky.
However much I try to look
the other way, the ice is melting
and the tide keeps rolling in.

## Please Beguile My Smile

I grin, like the teeth of the Cheshire cat
when all the furry bits have gone.
While, all around this strange tableau,
there is no time
to wander on.

## Being Human

I, myself, undo,
because to be with you: my aim,
undoes the well-fed reticence
that keeps me in my place, and tame.

I am not quite a picture card
and still afraid of trumps
which might add to my history
of secret wounds and bumps.

I'm used to hiding
as the pack howls by.
I've tied myself in daisy chains, and think
that half-way up the hill is high.

Perhaps enough,
for I am also
half-way down the sky,
waiting for passing nightingales
to show me how to fly;

Or teach me to sing
one immortal song
that I may tweet
before I die.

## Deconstructing

Meaning comes
when words bare bums
and are not chained
predictably.

And so let go
safe hands
and wave aflame
in brilliance.

Speak lonely
for yourself
and fly
beyond the anywhere,
to stumble by
the rippling stars
that touch and whizz
according to their moods
to find no when or why.

And thus glide ever new,
wallowing through hues,
transformed by every kiss of air,
to ever-changing everywhere.

## A Look At Life

I wipe a tear away
and find that I've
erased my eye,
and when I blink,
the plug is pulled
inside the sink
and down I go,
transformed to tears
which shower down the drain
to glitter out in wind,
like stars,
some witch
has frozen
into snow.

The windscreen-wipers
wipe me to and fro
until the screen is blank,
and where and who
I ever was
no being can know.

For never was a being
that thought it was,
more than a thought that has
no other place to go.

## Epilogue*

...and then ...

the total joy

of nothing

at all

awakes me

with a smile

... again...

*Written in 17 beats,
that slipped away
from the traffic lights
on the Haiku's narrow streets.

*Afterword:*     Why Poetry?

Long before words were written down, songs and poetry were there.

First there were words evolved from sounds of pain, pleasure, shock, or excitement, and then came names for things, people and actions, to make the beginnings of language; and thus it grew.

But in the background there were also the songs of birds, the calls of animals, and, most persistently, the sounds of weather, in thunder, wind and the beat of rain.

And because man must have water, it would surely have been the first natural instrument, with the splash and song of streams, the fall of waves, or the drawn out rattle of shingle, or slurp of sands, as they retreat and rise.

Each of us has a drum in our chest and the rhythms of our breath are ever present to govern our movements and our speech. So keeping the beat and dancing is natural, and must have come hand in hand with clapping and slapping, and drumming wherever sticks could be found to tap on wood or rocks.

Thus music and grunts could come together to make some kind of chant. You could hum along, or improvise sounds with your lips and tongue, until some new-found words dropped in, to mix with these tunes and rhythms and make songs.

Such communications are special: not only because they bring folk together in a social act, but also because they stick in the memory. And thus they became the vehicle for carrying the identity of the people, its myths and its history.

Where prose is very hard to recall line by line, nearly everyone can sing hundreds of songs, and many can quote pieces of poetry; largely because it has patterns, like assonance, rhythm and rhyme, which make a music that holds it together, and tells us that "this is a poem".

But lately things have changed, as rhythms and forms have become subtler, and often seem to have disappeared. It sometimes seems that the poetry establishment has been kidnapped by a form of writing which reads like prose, but is split into three line segments, with gaps between to suggest they are verses, and therefore make poems. But this can be hard to accept.

Such 'poems' may contain powerful images, strong statements and interesting ideas, presented boldly or in a sequence that is more striking than the continuity and logic of other prose, but often they miss the subtle rhythms and style of modern masters like T.S.Eliot, Ted Hughes, Robert Frost, or R.S.Thomas, and lacking the patterns that have made poetry for thousands of years, who will remember them? Have they any chance of being borne, like ancient sagas, from generation to generation without the need for writing?

Perhaps it's enough to have them recorded, so we may walk with earphones, since they are unlikely to spring to mind, line by line, as life goes on.

But this is not good enough for me. As a poet I am gripped by the music and rhythm of words, and cannot escape them. In everything I write, I feel these rhythms, but especially in poetry. And when I break them, by carelessness, they stick in my craw.

Therefore I hope you too may share the joy and excitement I get from these sounds, and some of those you find in this book may stay with you to sing in your mind and bring you some joy or a pause for thought, even when books and talking machines are left behind.

## Kevan Myers...

... was born, and lived a while, in London; then took off, thumbing his way to many lands; and now that planes are cheap, he always bags a window seat, hoping for cloudless skies to show the ground below, where still, his itchy feet have dreams to spread their toes..

In 1967, he set off to round the World, but got waylaid, in Punjab, sitting backwards on a horse-cart, faced by setting sun which spread across the skies, between the trees; accompanied by clopping hooves and birds with wild cries.

He found that India had grabbed his hand and when he dared to think to leave, she wouldn't let him go.

He tried twice more to round the globe, but every time she mugged him on the road, and stole his watch, and spun him round, then dragged him to a holy place, deep in the South, where, by some grace, he found the place to plant some trees and build the house where he would stay, for many years. And even now it still remains his winter refuge, far from the cold and damp of Northern climes.

But other seasons brought a heat that baked him too much, and at those times, he fled to where the Himalayan peaks look down from high at hilly feet. Then on he went to places, cool and distant, like Alaska, which held him amazed for two summers. But the next one, he opted to try out Europe again.

He set off exploring the back roads of France in a motor-home, which carried him one day to an odd-shaped house, with a gorgeous view, on terraces beneath the kind of tower, where Rapunzel dwells ,on the edge of a rough-hewn granite village, deep in the forested, hills of Corrèze.

And there he now resides most of the year, enjoying his time with new-found friends, helping to inspire and organise the writers' group, where many of these poems first saw life.

Between these times, in other lands, he worked in
schools, in Britain and in Denmark, trying to teach
the words and tools that make it possible to speak the
feelings and the thoughts which make each being
unique.

Of course he learnt as much from those he taught as
they found out from him. And still their unchanged
souls will bring him smiles on frequent visits to his
thoughts and dreams.

But other moments may deliver nightmares where he
panics in his mind, pursued by time, unable to recall
his teaching plans and gather up his stuff, till suddenly
he wakes up, half-way to a class, completely in the buff.

He's much relieved that he escaped in time; as
governments turned classrooms into prisons, where
each move must be pre-planned and given marks, for
fear that raging fires might spring from any stray
creative sparks.

It's now a long time since he left, with few regrets and
now he lives a different life in each one of his homes.

In France he's glad to shower with hot water, park
himself in comfy chairs and eat and drink too much.

But India remains the place which feeds his soul, and
heals his body from the excess of the West, with simpler
food, and ancient cures, which send him back more
youthful than he came.

And while he's there you'll find him still, inside or near,
the round and simple house, he built, beside the holy
mountain, in that climate where his windows never
close and sleeping can take place, near to the breathing
trees and stars, which peer through the mosquito net, to
light his face.

Other Poetry from Kevan Myers,
also available:

Salvage From The Ark (1978)

Tasting The Spring Where Pictures Sing (2006)

Is (2009)

To place orders for these books,
email: dancingyeti@gmail.com
where Kevan Myers welcomes
contact, thoughts and criticism.

There is also a Facebook page:
'Kevan Myers: poems and thoughts'

*Author's photo, copyright © Jim Lemkin 2018*

www.ingramcontent.com/pod-product-compliance
Lightning Source LLC
Chambersburg PA
CBHW070911080526
**44589CB00013B/1260**